Feelings are Fickle
and Other Things I Wish
Someone Had Told Me

Listen. I wish I could tell you it gets better.
But, it doesn't get better.
You get better.

— Joan Rivers

This book is for Gina
who has already figured out
many things I need more time for.

Author's Note:

Any reference to time across the book "a month ago, a week ago", respects when the essay was written.

Contents

Things I Wish
Someone Had Told Me
About My Own Evolution

How Is It Possible That I Exist?

Hundreds and thousands of things — millions of things — had to line up just right.

Galaxies and their trajectory. Stardust and how it fell. Evolution and the way it took place across eons. People encountering other people, so they could get together and make the people who made the people who made the people who made me.

My mother and father meeting for the first time in that field of poppies.

The moment of my conception — not earlier or later. Not to any other people but these two people, complete with their fire and their dreams.

My existence defies all odds.

I am a miracle, and so are you.

3

How Do You Right the Wrongs of the Universe?

I am full of flaws.

I am a part of the universe.

To right the wrongs of the universe, I start with me.

Are You Supposed to Figure Out Your Own Meaning of Life?

Imagine you are given a stupendous gift.

I don't know. A penthouse. A brand new car. A diamond ring. A plane ticket to the place of your dreams.

Now imagine if that gift came with a catch.

You can keep the penthouse only if you live in it with me. You can only drive the car if I am in the passenger seat. You can't wear the ring unless you're not with me. This plane ticket is yours, but I get to say where you go and what you pack.

The best gifts have no conditions.

Someone somewhere decided to give me the gift of life. Here, this is yours. You decide what to do with it.

At Peace With What I Can Do

When I started doing yoga I was very stiff.

Every pose seemed difficult — many seemed impossible.

Poses considered "resting poses", such as child's pose, did not feel like resting poses to me.

It was hard to stick with yoga because I found everything about it frustrating, like a struggle with myself.

I needed to learn how to drop the struggle.

It helped a lot to understand that the point was not the pose, or to do what others were doing, or to achieve anything (such as increased flexibility) but to accept me for exactly where I was at.

The pose is not what others do — the pose is what I can do. This often requires adjustments or the use of props.

I started going to class almost every day (five times a week).

In about two weeks I felt differently. Calmer, but also I could detect improvements in my flexibility.

In two months these became more obvious.

In about a year I was doing things I never thought I could.

I've now been doing yoga pretty regularly for about nine years. On most days I can do very showy poses — headstands, handstands, arm balances — but if I am standing up straight and do a forward fold, I cannot touch my toes.

I use blocks to bring the floor closer to me and put my hands on the blocks instead of on the floor.

I stay focused on my own effort and my own trajectory and don't even consider comparing myself to others.

The fact that I am at peace with what I can do rather than struggle to achieve a certain pose — or struggle to achieve what the person next to me is doing — is to me one of the many, many great things yoga has given me.

Left Out

It's awful to feel left out. I want to be invited to everything even when most of the time I really like being home alone.

It's not so much that I want to go to everything. I just want to feel like I'm included.

This expectation is, of course, impossible. Friends, even dear ones, sometimes go ahead and plan things without me. It would be irrational for me to even try to change this.

I spend some time with me and take a good look at what I would really, really like to be doing.

I set aside all the things I am supposed to consider fun and select the ones that are fun for me.

No to parties or large groups of people. No to drinking. Yes to going on a hike, to wandering down a new street where I can window shop and look at things, yes to bookstore visits and small dinners and tea for two.

Yes to museums, to an exhibit I want to see, a new city to visit, a new person to meet.

Yes to people I truly want to spend more time with. No to people whose company I don't actually enjoy.

8

Then, I organize my own activities and either go by myself (bliss) or populate them with people I enjoy.

I organize a dinner for six people who don't know each other and watch how they exchange numbers and become friends. I invite a friend I haven't seen on a hike so we can talk. I stroll across a museum alone with no one telling me to either wait or hurry.

The more I fill my life with people I really want to be with doing things I really want to do, the less likely I am to ever feel left out.

Things We Say to Avoid Responsibility

I don't know what I want.

I don't know where I'm going.

This was not my fault.

This was your fault.

Someone is trying to screw me.

I am too old/ young/ unlucky/ lazy/ tired/busy/confused.

Life is so unfair.

I am not interested.

I didn't have a choice.

I have no control.

I was asked to do this.

I was following orders.

That's too hard.

I can't.

I don't want to.

I can't risk that.

I don't trust you.

I don't trust myself.

I am a victim — I always have been.

Nobody understands me.

Nobody likes me.

Everyone hates me.

No one wants to help me.

Silence

Silence is the absence of noise.

That's it.

It's not good or bad, positive or negative. It's not a friend or a foe. It's not a catastrophe or something to overcome. It just is.

I can legitimately attribute anything I want to it, look:

Silence is dark, awkward, uncomfortable, heavy, oppressive.

Silence is blue, peaceful, calm, quiet, still, tranquility.

If I find silence awkward it's not what it is but what I bring to it. I am allowing something neutral to become a reflection of my insecurity.

If there is a pause in conversation and I decide I need to fill it, an innocuous pause becomes a gaping one, makes me restless, anxious, panicked.

If I decide silence is peaceful and a welcome oasis in a world full of noise I remain calm, smile, listen, sip my tea, wait a beat.

I resist the urge to flounder.

When silence gently comes over a conversation, I take a breath. This moment will reveal a confident me or an anxious me.

It's not silence I am afraid of. It's the part of me it will expose.

Don't Fake It Till You Make It

Faking something implies deceit. You are appearing to be something you're not. It's a trick.

I would much rather represent who I am or what I am really feeling.

Sometimes I don't have things figured out. Sometimes I don't know what I am doing. Sometimes I feel afraid. Sometimes I need help.

How am I going to be receptive to learning if I am busy acting like I know?

How will I be open to support or guidance if I am creating the illusion that I don't need it?

How can I establish trust if I am dissimulating?

"Fake it till you make it" is terrible advice. You can't expect to accomplish anything real through pretending.

Hatred

Hatred is passion. It's a feeling, intense and hostile and extreme. It's loathing, and it's a part of me trying to tell me something. That this is wrong, or unfair. That it wasn't supposed to be this way.

Life is full of messengers bearing important announcements. I try to be aware of these messengers, in particular the ones that come in unexpected disguises.

I try to recognize these messengers for what they are, take them in. Listen to them. I try to pay attention. Despite the discomfort or pain, they are here to guide me.

Hatred can be toxic but this happens only when I try to shut it down, judge it or reject it.

If I had an important message to convey and I kept getting turned away or told I was disgusting I too would be incensed.

It's a good policy to try to treat everything with kindness.

Even my hatred.

In most cases, she is just afraid.

How Do I Stop Making
the Same Mistake?

I love sugar. I try to eat less of it but it's so hard.

You know why it's hard? It's not just that it's addictive and delicious. It's that I associate it with a reward.

I deserve it, because I've been good.

Telling myself I can't have sugar doesn't work for my brain. I tell her instead that she has been so good and hard working she deserves something healthy.

This sense that I am nurturing instead of depriving myself is not infallible but it works much better.

To stop making the same mistake, it helps for me to stop working on the mistake itself, which is just a consequence.

Instead, I see if I can find the root cause of why I do what I do, and try to alter that.

Constant Disarray

Anxiety wants proof that it deserves to exist.

It wants to feel important. It wants you to feel you cannot survive without it.

Anxiety is a relentless sense of distress. It's unease, restlessness, tense and gnawing.

It puts my system in a state of flight or fight whether or not I'm in the presence of danger.

If I am anxious all the time, obviously some of the things I am anxious about will take place.

That's what happens when I'm anxious about everything.

Anxiety is exhausting. It is extremely unhealthy.

Anxiety comes from inside of me. It flares up from a thousand stories I spin. It is not a reflection of reality.

If I tell myself that anxiety is a form of foreshadowing, if I believe my anxiety is precognition, a form of extrasensory perception, telepathic, that's a trap.

In an effort to live a more peaceful life it's very hard to let go of something I am convinced can see the future. The unspoken lie is *"if I let go of my anxiety, I will not be safe."*

My anxiety cannot see the future. Nothing can. The future has not taken place and as such cannot be divined by my nervous system.

My intent with this is not to diminish what I feel (or what you feel). I am not suggesting you not trust your intuition.

It's just that living in a state of constant internal disarray is very painful and I prefer to let the truth (my anxiety cannot see the future and as such it's OK to let it go) set me free.

How Can I Create My Ideal Life?

An ideal life is not something I create, as this would assume life is static, fixed, like a butterfly I can pin and mount inside a glass case.

Life is instead something I practice and work at. I change, and the people around me change, and the circumstances around it all change, and I do the best I can to adjust as I go.

For periods of time my life is in a good place and then I realize one day that alterations need to be made.

For periods of time my life is in a place that is not so good.

I keep practicing: with the choices I make, the decisions I make, and the prioritizing and re-prioritizing I exercise to make sure I am paying attention to the right things.

Everything is always in motion, which means anyone's best life can begin at any time, even if up until now you feel you have not been living it.

Ambivalence

I would like to be at total ease with my own ambivalence.

I am not referring to hesitation or doubt but rather an internal clash of absolutes.

Despite having a personality many would call categorical, my stance, my preferences and my choices have a tendency to fluctuate or contradict themselves.

I frequently experience a mad desire to do and not do, to want and not want, right and wrong, yes and no, at the same time.

I want to learn how to hold this ungraspable, uncomfortable "everything" rather than the arbitrary "I have to decide," because ambivalence — also known as contradiction, incongruence or "lack of closure" — is more real to me than the fallacy of "putting things to rest".

How Can I Get What I Want?

I wanted to get in shape — really, I did — but whenever I came across a cookie I would eat it.

It turned out I aspired to get into shape, but every time I was given a choice, I proved to myself I wasn't willing to do what it would take.

I noticed there was a difference between a vague aspiration — let's call it a whim — and a true want.

For example, a relationship. I wanted to be with someone, but, men. Ugh.

I aspired to a grown up relationship but it was so much easier to keep blaming others for whatever wasn't working out, and then wondering why on earth I was so attracted to unavailable men.

I know full well that many, many times no matter what I do, no matter how hard I work, I will not get what I want.

But I also know that if there is any chance that I can, the very first step to take is to align myself internally.

I make sure that I really want what I say I want, rather than acting like I want one thing while pursuing another.

Do You Care People Think You're Weird?

Oh my god of course I care.

It hurts!

Honestly, given the choice I would much rather you think I'm impressive and brilliant and maybe even beautiful.

I can't not care. This is in part because I'm vain and love to be admired, but mostly because being liked made us more likely to survive and as such we are wired to search for approval.

It's almost impossible to alter a primal, original design.

The issue is that if I listen to that voice inside of me that wants me to do something so that you like me, I will chase something uncatchable forever because there is nothing — and I mean nothing — I can do that everyone can agree is likable.

No matter what I do there will always be people who don't approve. Or who judge. Or who criticize.

Or (and this is both the worst and the most frequent occurrence) who don't care enough to even think, much less talk about me.

And in the process of chasing something I already know is uncatchable, I will lose myself.

Why Is Being Materialistic Bad?

Deriving pleasure from stuff is superficial and fleeting but also it breeds insatiability. It's never enough. Or new enough. Or cool enough.

It's easy for others to have more, better stuff, or something you don't yet have, so you are always comparing yourself to people around you and feeling angsty over what you might be lacking.

This, instead of paying attention to what you already have.

This is the optimal recipe for unhappiness.

What happens if you are always comparing what you have against what others have? Instead of the sense that you are lucky and that you have everything you need you invite envy, greed, jealousy, a sense that nothing is fair.

You begin to measure yourself and others by things. Everything feels incomplete.

If you define yourself by outside things your attention is diverted from inside things: emotions, qualities, principles, values, common sense.

You end up with a house full of stuff you don't need and a soul that feels starved and doesn't understand why.

I mean, why, if I have everything?

The Other Is Like You

One of the most painful things is the illusion that we are alone and that no one understands us. Compassion is the antidote.

Compassion is an ability to put yourself in another person's shoes. It means you can see things from their perspective — it's a deep form of understanding.

Compassion makes it much more difficult to feel indifference and isolation. It makes it harder to feel anger, frustration, animosity.

It invites you to realize that another is like you. It lends you a feeling of community instead of one of disassociation.

Compassion gets you out of your troubles and your stories and your head, to connect you, introduce you to a collective instead of individual universe.

Being compassionate is one of the ways to move through the world understanding more and suffering less.

Self-Confident

A self-confident person:

Can distinguish reality from her insecurity. For example: I don't need to get everything perfect, I don't need to compare myself to others, I know that when I feel nobody understands me I have to work on understanding myself.

Feels gossip and putting others down is a waste of time and cannot be bothered with it.

Knows who she is and what she wants. This is because the need for approval does not override her own voice.

She is transparent. She expresses what she thinks and what she likes. She is not afraid of not being liked for who she is so she has nothing to hide.

She craves time alone. She does not need to be constantly distracted and feels like being alone = being in the best company.

She treats herself well. She is her own best friend. Her inner narrative is kind.

She takes care of herself. She eats well, goes to the doctor, does things she enjoys as a gift to herself.

She does healthy things. Goodbye, toxic relationships (even if I still love you). Goodbye, job where I'm not appreciated. I deserve better, and I'm going to go find it.

She recognizes her own efforts. Even if no one knows the effort she just went through, she knows. She feels proud of herself.

Beautiful Mistakes

Regret is wishing I had not done that. It is a sense of remorse.

I don't want to diminish regret. It's absolutely awful to feel you did something you can't take back.

But if you design your life to avoid regret then you diminish your experiences, your ability to learn, to test yourself and to grow.

By all means exercise caution. In particular be careful when it comes to the feelings of others.

That being said, I don't believe avoiding things on the grounds they might be painful later is a sound way to go through life. You might miss out on the most beautiful mistakes.

Torment and Butterflies

I am talking to a friend and she is in her late twenties and she — you know. She worries. She worries about so many things.

I know exactly how she feels. And I do mean exactly. Because, I was twenty just a few weeks ago, and because in most ways I am in my twenties now.

I lean back in my chair and I am listening but also I am thinking about all the things I want to say.

What I want to say is *oh my god. Oh my god just look at you. You have everything you need.*

You are beautiful in ways you won't understand for decades. You are in a hurry, but have so much time. You feel like you will have everything figured out a few years from now but all you are doing is rushing towards the time you realize that moment never comes.

And your angst — ah, your angst. I know you want to get rid of it, and you should, but also it's life force. Use it.

I was not like you when I was in my twenties. You are so together. You see so much more than I ever did.

You are going to be OK. I don't mean everything is going to be OK. I mean you. I know this because I see it right in front of me, plain as day.

That's what I want to say, but I don't bother. This is because she is sitting there, precious, tangled, all torment and butterflies, and I already know she will not believe me.

Is Optimism Delusional?

This question assumes that pessimists see things as they are. This puts me in a place where I would have to accept detaching myself from reality in order to be happy, where I have to decline seeing things clearly if what I want is to feel good.

How can I possibly be happy if I believe happiness is a bargain I would never want to strike?

I reject any perspective that traps me into having to choose not to be happy, or that makes me believe that happiness implies the loss of something I can't live without.

Instead, I can be happy without ever needing to deceive myself, and so can you.

Is Guilt Good or Bad?

You feel guilty.

Are you paralyzed, ashamed, in pain, beating yourself up, trapped? Is your view of the world distorted, irrational, anxious, diminished, polluted? Do you hate yourself, because, ugh, how could you?

Or, does this sense of guilt serve to regulate your behavior, as a voice from your conscience? Is it something fleeting, that flares up but then clears out, informs future decisions so you become a better person?

Guilt is neither good or bad. It depends on what you do with it, and what it does to you.

Space for Grief

Loss is indivisible from life. They come together, intertwined, often indistinguishable.

Fact: I will some day lose everything I now have, everything, even things I consider immutable.

"Immutable". What a fool.

This is why my body comes equipped with a precious, primal, fundamental way to process loss: grief.

Grief is how I sort out my new reality, how I learn to do without whatever it is that I used to consider indispensable.

Taking grief away from me by demanding that I be happy, that I cheer up, that I buck up, that *come on, it's been long enough, let's go do something fun*, is an assault on the only way I have to accept this enormous thing that I have lost.

My life will never be the same.

If you don't give me room to move through this I will be stuck forever in this place of darkness.

Grief needs to take place. It needs to be respected. It needs space. It needs support.

Slow down. Lower your voice. Lower your head. Wear dark clothes. Leave me alone.

I am saying goodbye.

Do not suffocate grief unless you want the person suffering through it to remain broken forever.

How Do You Know It's Time to Change?

I get up early every morning to write.

The time is the same. The place is the same. The computer is the same.

The only thing that changes from one day to the next is me.

Some days I write a lot. I feel connected, inspired.

Some days I have trouble pushing through even a few sentences.

How I feel about what I write is my canary in the mine.

If for too many days my writing feels stuck, like I can't get inspired, like I have all this life all around me and yet I don't know what to say, I know it's time to change something.

Permanence

I eat even if I know I will again be hungry.

I pour myself a cup of coffee even when I know the outcome will be an empty cup.

I read even if I know I will forget.

I write and I don't even know if anyone will read this.

I have sex despite being sure I will want to again.

I do things that bring me pleasure even if I know this delicious thing is fleeting.

I build, and I know this will crumble.

Permanence does not exist. How fortunate that it's not why we do things.

What Does Nobody Tell You About Adult Life?

Being an adult is glorious. You have a car and a credit card and the one who gives you permission is you.

Sex gets better. If you think it's fun in your twenties, just wait and see what's in store for you.

Everyone will judge you, but nobody cares. Think about that the next time you let what others think determine what you decide to do.

Love does not conquer all. It's actually quite fragile.

There are many, many battles you cannot win with optimism or "the right attitude".

Sometimes you won't be happy. Sometimes everything will suck.

There is no such thing as your soul mate or your other half. Stop looking for something that doesn't exist.

The more comfortable you are alone, the better your relationships.

The more open you are, the less vulnerable.

Feelings are fickle.

Thoughts are just thoughts.

Your perception is not reality.

Your opinion is not a fact.

Your expectations will sink your relationships. They will sink you.

You will have less of whatever you chase.

Waiting is a form of inaction. Don't confuse it with a virtue.

Action begets motivation — not the other way around.

Disappointment is an inside job. So is happiness.

Blame is a decoy. You do things to yourself.

You will betray yourself.

A white lie is a lie.

Your purpose is not something you find.

The time when you have it all figured out does not exist.

The point when you become an adult does not exist.

Everything changes.

Nothing is yours to keep.

You are going to die. So is everyone you love.

The meaning of life is up to you.

If Feelings Are Fickle, Why Act on Them?

Many, many feelings come and go. They are a flash, lightning, brush fire, forest fire, a cleanse, nothing.

Many feelings come and direct your life. They are a guiding light, a lighthouse, a bright shooting star, everything.

You can tell the difference because aside from feelings you have thoughts, and aside from thoughts you have goals.

You come with other things too: ethics, principles, intentions, your decisions, your actions — a sense of right and wrong.

Feel a feeling. Think a thought. Give each their just, fair space. Let them take you for a spin — you might as well, since they will whether you want them to or not.

But recognize that just because you feel something doesn't mean you must act on it.

What do you want? Where will following this feeling take you? Does that sound like somewhere you want to go? Does that sound like the person you want to be?

You are not your feelings. You are the person who feels them. You are not your thoughts. You are the person who thinks them.

What you are is the person who gets to decide.

How Do You Work Through Envy?

Envy is the desperate, bitter, gnawing sense that I want what someone else has.

It does two sneaky things:

It forces my intense focus on the other, when the issue is in me. This is like trying to heal my broken arm by setting the cast on someone else's arm.

Then, it forces my attention on what the other has, reminding me of what I don't have instead of what I do have.

It *feels* like the way to heal envy is to think about how to get what I am coveting.

The problem is that in the presence of this insatiable appetite that is envy, there will always be something more to want.

Instead, what I need to do is turn the attention on me.

What am I really lacking that makes me feel like I want what someone else has?

Then I need to focus my attention on all the things I do have, realize how much that is, how fortunate I am, and how much better it feels to exercise gratitude (soothing, joyful, true) for what I have rather than greed (scratching, ravenous, false) for what I don't.

To many, many vexations of the spirit, gratitude is the antidote.

What if Someone Breaks a Promise?

Promises are important. We want them because they feel like assurance, a guarantee in a turbulent world.

I don't want to make any less of anyone's word of honor.

Promises are also intractable. They are inflexible, cannot be bent.

In this world, what survives the longest is what yields, what is pliable, what is capable of adaptation.

I am happiest when I recognize I can promise nothing, when I ask others not to promise me anything, when from the beginning rather than demanding something rigid I accept other people as fallible.

Does Meditation Improve Me?

It's easy for me to believe that improvement, perfection and happiness are somewhere else. *As soon as I find someone to share my life with. As soon as I land the right job. As soon as I lose 5 more pounds.*

This moving, running, always grasping for something just beyond my reach is exhausting.

Meditation is a rest from that. It's sitting with everything that is.

You, wild and imperfect. You, uncomfortable and scared. You, twitchy and overwhelmed with all the thoughts you can't stop thinking.

Just sit. Just breathe. Not to feel better, not to get better, not to overcome.

It's just about paying attention. That's it.

How Do I Switch From Fear to Thrill?

This question makes it sound like there is a hidden switch somewhere that can be flipped.

If only someone could just tell me where it is.

In my personal experience there is no such switch. There is no eliminating fear, no exchanging it for a thrill.

Instead it's a practice, an every day facing off with my fear. *Look. I know you are not aiming for me to lead a dull, small life. You are in fact trying to keep me safe. But surely you see we have to try this, right? Come on. Come with me. Let's go.*

And so I don't smother or fight off the fear but rather soothe it and acknowledge it and keep it around as an ally and a valuable voice in my decision-making process.

It's not the boss of me but I recognize it can make a valuable contribution. It needs to feel involved and important.

I repeat this, every day, and over time fear starts shrinking and new things become more exciting because I have my own experience as proof that I got through them.

There is no switch. There is no off button for fear. It was put there for a reason and if you try to eliminate it it will turn into a monster.

Emotions really do not take well to being ignored, fought against or extinguished. They like being seen, recognized and valued, just like you and me.

Everyone Around Me

It's very common to feel like "everyone around me" is doing something I'm not a part of.

"Everyone around me" is in some way leaving me out of something.

"Everyone around me" has their life together.

"Everyone around me" likes this and does not like that.

"Everyone around me" has a life that's better than mine.

"Everyone around me" is better than me.

I am missing out because "everyone around me" does cooler stuff than the stuff I do.

If I do that, what will "everyone around me" think?

In order to succeed — or at the very least be happier and at peace — the first step is to know that any version of "everyone around me" is a lie.

Celebrate

I am a big, big celebrator of my small victories.

Do you know why?

Because every day I accomplish things that are super easy for you and super difficult for me.

You simply cannot know the effort I put behind something that you do without thinking, and as such cannot appreciate what I just overcame.

The same holds true for you: you fight a thousand secret battles that are incredibly challenging for you and that seem second nature to others.

People cannot commend you for what they can't see.

So make sure you celebrate your victories, those invisible acts of courage, that gigantic yet imperceptible effort that only you know about. No one else can.

The only person in the whole world who knows about what is indiscernible to us but a gigantic leap for you is you. Brave, heroic you. Hurray for you!

Should I Listen to Myself or Others?

Listening to others instead of to me (rather than in addition to me) quickly impairs my ability to believe that what I am telling myself is valuable.

My instincts become too tenuous for me to hear them.

I become unable to answer simple questions. *How are you? How do you feel? Are you OK?*

What do you want to do with your life?

I should not need someone else's opinion to answer these questions. I should not need to be told what the truth about what I want is.

If I find myself in this position I step away from others and from outside noise until I become audible to myself again.

There is no guarantee that what I tell myself is infallible. But I'd rather live with the consequences of my mistakes than with someone else's version of a life that belongs only to me.

How Do I Live a Life Equal to the Gift of Life?

Spend most of your time creating something.

Love.

Experience the entire range of every emotion that presents itself.

Reject the notion that anything revolves around you. Believing that anything does is the quickest way to become unendurably boring.

Don't mind criticism.

Be an active part of communities you contribute to building.

Listen, and read. Those two are very similar.

Cultivate a beginner's mind.

Forever divorce pleasure from guilt.

Accept.

Be easily enraptured.

Fall madly in love with impermanence. Now that's something you can count on.

Play with plants and animals and realize you cannot disassociate from nature.

At least once a week, power down. Computer. Phone. Brain. If you are really busy, make that twice a week.

Make certain every one of your senses is regularly, deliberately put to use. When was the last time you ran your feet across something scratchy?

Treat your body as if it was sacred, because it is. But remember it likes being used in all the ways nature intended.

Go find happiness. It's OK if it takes the rest of your life.

Wimp

I consider myself to be categorically pragmatic and a total wimp.

This means that my outlook is practical, but it also means I don't want to suffer so I consider things from all angles and deliberately choose the one likely to make me suffer less.

I am a happier person as a result.

Things Come and Go

When I was a teenager an adult who had authority over me told me that I was fickle, and that my future depended on my ability to commit to one thing.

I know he meant well, but now that I'm an adult I can tell you that what made my life rich and interesting was a broad-ranging curiosity. I had, and still have, many interests. I have nothing against deep specialization, but being eclectic is just as valuable.

It's equally valuable, in different ways.

This same well-intentioned person told me I couldn't develop a passion over something and then just abandon it. But I can and did — I still do. I tend to go all in, but that doesn't mean I go all in forever. I feel passionate about something and then lose interest. It's not even because I'm mercurial — it's because many things run their course, and because — and I don't mean to be flip, but factual — most things are temporary.

Don't get me wrong. Living life bound to a single passion is cool too. What I object to — what I categorically object to — is the notion that there is a formula. A hard and fast rule that has to work for everyone.

Please be who you are. Honor your passion and ride it forever, or just ride it out. Be committed to what you decide to pay attention to, but don't hold on too tightly. Things come and go. It's what they do. The natural order of things will not spell doom for you.

Do We Learn More From Pain or Pleasure?

Let's say that when you were very young the person responsible for taking care of you misused that role and diminished you in their attempt to discipline you.

This hurt you a lot and you would really rather not go through that pain again.

This leaves a code in your inner world. You now associate "authority" with "this is very bad news".

You go through life revolting against authority, even authority who wants to guide and teach and who has no intention of causing you harm.

We all have this code designed to protect us from what we now interpret as dangerous.

We need to be awake to make a distinction between our once useful, now obsolete codes and the true intent of the people who surround us.

Sometimes we have to unlearn what we learned from pain in a search for peace and to make our life more attuned to reality.

A "valuable lesson" is unrelated to pain and to pleasure.

Experience is about having the awareness to put what happens to us in its rightful place so that we recognize things for what they really are.

51

Does Failure Make Us Strong?

Failure does not necessarily make you strong.

Constant failure might not lead to success.

Nothing is "meant for you."

There are no formulas, rules or guarantees.

Venture instead into things that interest you to any degree and bring you any amount of pleasure.

Enjoy this moment right here.

It's all we've got.

Too Busy

When I first began taking yoga classes I was mortified about all the things I couldn't do.

What if people thought I was incompetent, inflexible, out of shape?

I noticed in the throes of my stress that I spent a great deal of energy worrying about how humiliated I could feel but no energy at all looking at others or thinking less of them because of what they could or could not do.

Be who you are. Do what you can. Follow what interests you. When you walk into any room and worry what others might think of you, let me assure you they are way too busy worrying about what others think of them.

What Skills Are Useful Every Day?

Observation: Be attentive. Notice. Nothing is ordinary.

A sense of adventure: Take a chance. Participate. Explore.

Resourcefulness: Exercise your ability to deal with an unexpected turn of events.

Patience: Resist irritation or restlessness when something takes longer or is more complicated than you thought it would be.

Spontaneity: Don't over-plan. Don't premeditate. Act on impulse.

Wonder: Marvel. Return to the time when you experienced awe.

Why Do We Grieve When Death Is Inevitable?

I think about this all the time.

If we know everybody dies we should be more prepared, more adroit at handling death's imminent arrival.

The best answer I can come up with is this: if I climb a tree and from the tallest branch I realize I will fall and break my arm, that will not lessen the pain of falling and breaking my arm.

Alas. The ability to anticipate pain is not an antidote to it.

My Path

The artificial, subjective sense of "not knowing what my path was" caused me a lot of distress. It placed a dirty, scratchy, disordered bale of disquiet in the center of my heart.

This was a story — *"I feel lost"* — and I confused my story with the truth.

One day I realized that certain things made me feel quite delighted and that I needed to do more of those things.

If I found my calling or not, what did it matter if I was full of wonder now?

Other things made me really miserable but even within that misery I always learned something, something that would invariably splatter light all over new things to feel wonder over.

I have realized that if I give more space, breathe more air and amp up anything that feels right and am receptive to learn from any and every experience life offers, then my path is everywhere.

My path is everywhere, and so is yours.

What Are the Top Five Best Decisions You Ever Made?

The day I decided many, many things were more important than being right.

The day I decided that even when it sure seemed like it, the things that happened in the swirling world around me were not about me.

The day I decided that I would stop complaining. *You don't like it, Dushka? Either fix it or accept it.*

The day I decided to assume everyone was doing the best they could. It didn't matter if this was true or not. It mattered that it shifted my perspective from being miffed to being compassionate.

The day I decided I would be full of tact and good intentions but never, ever lie. Not to "protect" someone, not to "make someone happy" not to save myself the effort of having to explain myself.

The day I decided I was not an uncanny, powerful mind reader and that if I needed to know what someone else was intending to do I could just ask.

The day I decided, after many years of requesting permission, waiting, consulting and asking, that the boss of my life was me.

What Are Some Things You Know Aren't True?

If you are lucky, really lucky, your parents will tell you *you are special*. And you are, you are. But not to everyone.

And it's not like it grants you a special pass, or special treatment.

If it does, it shouldn't.

You will make a best friend and she will say *BFF!* Let me tell you, forever is a long, long time.

And then your boyfriend vows to *always love you* and that will be a lie.

He's not deliberately lying. He thinks it's the truth. But he can't possibly know that.

Apply this to every earnest, full hearted promise. *I will always take care of you.* Can you know that? Can you really control that? No. No you can't.

Take care of yourself.

Next: all the things you are supposed to find. Purpose. Meaning. Your other half.

They are not out there waiting for you. You make things happen. You don't just find them.

58

Stop looking for something that doesn't exist.

Good things happen to those who wait. No. They don't. Don't sit around waiting.

You have a bright future and wonderful things are in store for you. You don't. They are not. Or maybe they are but they don't materialize. They don't appear.

Stop believing anything just because it makes things easy. Stop accepting whatever results in you being passive. Stop asking questions you should be answering.

Wake up. Take responsibility. Make your future. Create your wonderful things.

Why Do People Blame?

Because if I didn't do it I don't have to be responsible for it.

Because if it was you I don't have to change anything.

Because if it wasn't me I don't have to solve anything.

Because if it was you I can just complain, instead of dealing with growing up.

Because it's easier to lie than to tell the truth.

Because pointing the finger at you is a way to hurt you.

Because I have no idea why I did that and blaming you means I don't need to figure it out.

Because if I had nothing to do with it, I don't have to deal with the consequences.

Because if it's your fault and not my fault I don't have to ever think less of myself.

How to Change Anything

To tell you how to change anything, I am going to give you an answer that you will find massively unsatisfactory.

I know this because when I first discovered it I found it massively unsatisfactory.

Except that it has changed everything.

The answer is this: be aware. Aware. Like this: *"Wow. I am doing it again — I feel like this is someone else's fault."*

You don't judge it. It's not good or bad. You just see.

Once you become aware of something and identify it as damaging your body and your brain will begin to rearrange things. You don't need to understand how.

That's it. Awareness is the catalyst for everything.

What Sounds True but Isn't?

I feel a dazzling explosion of love for you. This means you feel it too.

You don't love me. This means I am unlovable.

You love someone else instead of me. This means I am not enough.

You cheated on me. This means you never loved me.

The more I plan, the more control I will have over my future.

The more control I exert over every painstaking detail, the more I will rule over the outcome.

The harder I work, the better I will do.

The more rational I am, the better my life will be.

It's better to make decisions than it is to wait.

The better my decisions, the better the outcome.

The wider and more sweeping my actions, the more drastically and surely things will change.

The more vigilant I am, the lesser the chances I will get betrayed.

The more vulnerable I become, the more I will get hurt.

When I get everything I want I will finally be happy.

Should I Start Working Out?

I once told my mom I wanted her help in eating a healthier diet. She made sure the food I wanted was available to me.

Then I hid from her the fact I was eating junk food at school.

One day she saw a bag of half eaten (vinegar) potato chips in my lunch bag. I told her they belonged to a friend.

She gave me an eye roll that put my entire teenage eye rolling experience to shame.

"Dushka," she said. *"I truly could not possibly care any less what you eat. You were the one who said you wanted to be healthier. Welcome to your life."*

What do you want? How do you suppose you will get there? If you don't do what it takes, who will have to live with the consequences of your actions, your choices, your decisions?

It's all you.

Welcome to your life.

Do You Ever Feel Like Giving Up?

Of course.

I'm so tired.

I can't do this anymore.

This may be the close cousin of *"I give up on everything".*

I think defying this feeling is where growth is.

Growing — evolving — hurts, and we want things to stay the same because that's more comfortable, so we resist it.

"Leave me alone" I want to say. *"Can't you see? I'm already doing everything I can."*

I guess the point is to defeat this sensation rather than let it defeat you.

Outdare it.

It's really hard. It takes more effort than you think you have to give.

But this is where resilience lives.

No Guarantees

Doing everything right (whatever that means) does not ensure a positive outcome.

Being in every way better than your competition does not imply you will win.

Academic excellence does not guarantee a successful life. Not even an average one.

Marriage does not clinch the end of heartbreak or your emotional salvation.

A promise — even a fervent, earnest one — does not secure its fulfillment.

I can instead assure you that many things you are certain of do not exist.

I guarantee an unpredictable life rife with unexpected twists and constant change.

Beyond that, the only helpful thing is how much time you've spent developing your own resilience and adaptation.

Unclench

The clutch of your fists.

The bite of your jaw.

The clench in any muscle.

The grasp so tightly coiled within your expectations.

The clamp of the fight you never had or the ones you did.

That casual thing he said that snagged your feelings.

The grip of that thing you did that you know you shouldn't have done.

The thoughts you grapple with or that grapple with you.

The hold he has on you.

The squeeze in your heart.

The clasp of that recollection.

The way you brace against things that never take place.

To any degree, in any measure, unclench something.

Why Is Grief the Only Emotion
With a Process?

Grief is not an emotion with a process.

Grief is a process — as personal as your fingerprint — with many, many emotions.

Grief contains darkness and sadness and isolation and changed my perception of time. I felt like the world was moving so fast while all I could do was stand there. I couldn't keep up. I could barely move.

But there are other things about grief that are harder to explain, even hard to talk about. For example, grief is filled with a beauty so piercing it takes my breath away even to remember it. And, it contains, or at least it did for me, such an enormous amount of relief that with each passing day, even after three years, I continue to feel progressively lighter.

I am shedding, shedding every day the weight that you were. That weight nearly crushed me.

Grief is inescapable. If you try to run it will be wherever you are running to, waiting for you. You have to let it move through you, the terror, the horror, the panic, the indescribable resplendence, the longing, the exuberance, the slice, the puncture, the release, the residue, the remains, the debris, the dreams, the nightmares, the desperate, desperate pacing, the grip. The vise grip. It will never let me go. I will never let you go.

I will miss you forever, but also, you are here. I know. I know.

What Stupid Thing Did You Do Today?

Sometimes I want something so much that I sabotage it so that I don't ever get it.

If I can ensure I will not get it then I don't have to stress about losing it or about the possibility that it might not happen.

Wow.

We Settle

You know what we do? We settle.

We find ourselves in a certain situation and convince ourselves this is what it's going to be.

(I feel trapped in my relationship, I've gained twenty pounds, I don't like my job, I feel a constant state of anhedonia or ennui.)

This is life. I can't change this.

Never, ever believe mediocrity, unhappiness or bleh is what you have to live with.

Things can always get better — even when they are good.

Identify what you should not have to be OK with and devise small steps to get out.

Do something that inches you closer to your escape every day.

Life can be absolutely amazing.

You just have to work at it.

Where Should I Spend More Time?

Every day I have a choice: to focus on big things or on petty things.

Petty things are safe and comfortable and dangerous because they give me the delicious illusion that I am busy.

Big things are scary and have me questioning my significance and my power.

But adding up all the petty things always equals nothing, and adding up big things marks the course of my life and what I — if only for a short period of time — leave behind.

No One Can Save You

This might hurt, but it's better that you know.

No one has the answers to your pressing life questions.

No one can help you.

No one has the fix you need.

No one will come save you.

And if someone does, and tells you things that sound like answers, they will lead you down the wrong path, not because they have any ill intent, but because they are not you.

When it comes to figuring out who you are and where you want to go, you're on your own.

If "on your own" sounds sad to you, one day it won't be.

You will soon come to see that it in fact means your life is in the very best hands.

I Don't Need That Anymore

When I was a little girl and acted impetuous, abrupt, demanding or aggressive, my mom would praise me. *"You,"* she would say *"are nobody's fool."*

As I grew older, if my actions were harsh, rash, fierce, she would beam. *"I pity whoever dares to cross you."*

My mom wanted me to be strong, to stand up for myself, to not let anyone walk all over her little girl.

Over the years, this got tangled up in me acting tough, trying, dictatorial, oppressive.

I could be a very difficult person, and felt that giving this up exposed me, made me weak, put me at risk of being taken advantage of.

It took me a long time to understand that you don't have to be mean or rude for others to be fair.

It was a guy I used to date who helped me unscramble this. One day he heard me on the phone talking to a customer service agent. I was frustrated, angry, despotic. When I hung up he asked me what on earth I was doing.

"I need to resolve this," I said. *"To resolve it, this is what I have to do."*

"Dushka, that's not true," he said. *"This person I just heard is not even who you are. Acting like that is so dramatically against your true nature that it depletes you. Look at yourself. You are unhappy, exhausted, disheveled. I don't even recognize you."*

This shook me. I thought about it for a long time. I hated this person that I became, but I needed to be her to be effective, to be heard, to be respected, to be safe, to get results.

Or did I?

I try to be someone I like. If I am ever not, it hurts me. If something hurts, it means it's all twisted up in something I believe in that isn't true.

Life is better when I identify and question that primal, original belief. It was programmed into me to keep me safe, but I don't need it anymore.

Fire

This morning I woke up feeling terribly anxious.

Why?

Who knows.

My brain doesn't like feeling anxious. She tried to fix everything.

"Get up," she said. *"Fill your day. Find distractions. Wow. This is really uncomfortable."*

"Wait a minute," I said. *"What are you afraid of? Why is this feeling so terrible?"*

I did something really difficult.

You know what I did? Nothing. I just lay there. I lay still in the dark.

You know what happened? Nothing. Nothing happened.

I had a few plans and I cancelled them.

I padded around in my apartment, sat in different chairs throughout the day, appreciated my soft rug and my things. I listened to the rain. Lit a candle. I put on lip gloss. I drank tea. I wrote.

My anxiety zipped around inside me like something electric and painful. I felt agony. Eventually, it settled down.

I've learned I can't run from my feelings. They are faster than me. If I sit still they swirl around me and feel heard and dissipate, sometimes in a few hours, sometimes longer.

This is what I do. I resist running. I resist distractions.

I resist above all attributing them to something outside of me. (I will feel better if he calls me/if I eat ice cream/if I buy something/if whatever.)

I just sit. I get still. This is not easy. It can feel like fire.

But then it's over.

I know this doesn't work for everyone, but it works for me.

Is a "Woman's Intuition" Always Right?

If you asked me to pick a word, just one word among hundreds of thousands, to most accurately describe humans, my choice would be "fallible".

We are fallible.

Nothing that comes from us is "always right".

There is so much lore around intuition, and around a woman's intuition.

Women are human. Intuition is human. It is not always right. Not even close.

I can state this with authority because I am a woman and because I frequently experience the rustling of my intuition.

Sometimes I'm right, and sometimes I'm not.

I completely trust myself, and trust that there is a possibility I might be wrong.

This has served me better than blindly trusting anything.

How Would You Be Different Without Pain?

As much as I would really love a life free of pain, I do concede that without it I would be less resilient, less adaptable, less independent, less appreciative, less grateful, less elastic with my perspective, less humble, less strong, more easily overwhelmed, less compassionate, less empathetic, less adroit at handing difficulty, and definitely less alive.

What Do Most People Feel but Nobody Talks About?

Oh shit my life, my life. My life is falling apart.

I have no clue what I am doing.

I am afraid I am not good enough.

I am terrified that I don't know what I want.

I worry all the time about what other people think.

I suspect I will never find love.

I worry I will never again find ____. (another job, another relationship, happiness)

I had a miscarriage and feel I am good for nothing.

I feel like something is missing from my life and I don't know what it is.

I don't know what my purpose is.

Someone abused me a long time ago and I have never told anyone because I was afraid — and still am — that no one will believe me.

I worry I am not normal.

I worry something is wrong with me.

I am surrounded by people and still feel lonely.

I have secrets — things that no one else has experienced.

I think everyone's life is better than mine.

How Do I Control My Emotions?

When I am sad or happy or excited, I say that's what I am.

Like this:

"I am sad." "I am happy." "I am excited."

But the fact is, I am not sad. I am me, and sad is just passing through.

I don't think it's possible to "control" your emotions, in particular because when you try to exert control over something you are giving it your full attention, which tends to make it bigger and stronger.

What helps is to not identify with your emotions. To make a distinction between what you feel and you.

As you separate who you are from what you feel, you start to become a witness to your feelings, instead of getting all tangled up with them. You recognize them as something powerful but transitory.

This makes it more plausible for feelings to move through you.

Hello, anger. You rock me to my core, but long after you sweep through me I will still be here.

I will outlast you, because you are not who I am.

81

Bad Habits

Expecting a lot from other people, then feeling crushingly disappointed.

Feeling crippling anxiety over I don't even know what.

Being terribly demanding of myself.

Exasperation. Impatience.

Taking things personally.

The assumption others can read my mind, or that I should be able to read theirs.

Believing the bullshit my ego comes up with (she is very creative).

Taking shallow breaths when I can take big ones whenever I want.

Getting completely carried away by my emotions.

Attempting to change another person.

Being sexually attracted to men who are not good for me.

Mistaking what everybody does for what I want.

Measuring my self-worth through approval or the absence of it.

Wanting things that I cannot have just because I cannot have them.

Difficulty believing my own perception.

Feeling like something I need can be found in someone else.

Dismissing my own feelings.

Experiencing normal passages of life as failures.

I work on these things every day. Because, the difference between a habit I can't break and one I overcome is practice.

What Do You Love About Yourself?

The fact that I love being alone is my favorite thing about me.

First, because it took me a long time to get to a place where it felt like a treat rather than lonely.

And second because of all the things I find when I am with myself: the answers to everything.

I wish I could give this to anyone who has ever felt isolated, lost or at a loss for what to do next: the pleasure of your own company.

I can't recommend you enough.

Do I Need Self-Control to Make or Break a Habit?

I don't like the term "self-control" because it makes me feel I am at war with myself.

Being at war with myself means I lose even when I win.

What I do is make a commitment to myself and keep it.

If I break it, instead of giving up on me I am patient and return to it.

I break it, and return to it.

When I break it I ask myself why. What happened? Was I tired, was I feeling overextended, did I not plan ahead?

What happened so that next time I can make it easier for myself? So that next time I can give me what I need to make this successful?

Sooner or later, the habit sticks.

Thank You

Every day I am bombarded with the message that I am not enough and that I don't have enough.

I need to be more, be better, or I will be left behind.

Everyone's life is better than mine. Everyone has more than me.

I will be happier as soon as I get ___.

Exercising gratitude shifts this perspective, from all the things I don't have or can't reach to all the things I already have. To all the reasons why I am one of the most fortunate people on the planet.

Change your perspective, change your life.

Wild Animal

If I had no feelings I would be cement. A discarded, dull piece of metal. Drywall. Lint.

I would never be amused. I would never be blissful. I would not ever feel proud or rapturous. I would not understand luxury. I would never feel exulted. I would not know wonder or satisfaction. I would never be perplexed.

I would not ever know this wild animal who lives inside my chest that sometimes sighs deeply and is so still and other times uses her nails and her teeth to rip out of me.

It would suck to have no feelings. I welcome the sorrow and the misery. I welcome the work and the woe. I welcome the grief.

I even welcome remembering that I will never see him again.

If I'm Lonely and Call a Friend Am I Avoiding Myself?

To me, the answer is about self-compassion.

I want to grow and as such am willing to be uncomfortable, but what if instead of discomfort and disquiet I am actually feeling a sense of despair or a gnawing pain?

I call a friend. I visit my family.

I love myself. I want to evolve and become stronger but I will not make myself suffer more than I need to.

In a sense it's like taking care of the small child version of me.

I want you to be resilient but I would never hurt you.

What Do You Know That Could Improve My Life?

Every decision you make is a brick in the wall of who you are. Everything you do matters.

Everyone will judge you, but nobody cares. Don't let what others think determine what you do.

Love does not conquer all. It doesn't even conquer simple things. Take care of it as you would something very fragile, because it is.

"Reliable" is much better than "thrilling". "Reliable" is hotter than "sexy". "Solid" and "nice" are vastly underrated.

There is no such thing as your soul mate. Stop looking for something that doesn't exist. Start creating what you want.

Intimacy is not built by someone confiding in you. It's built by someone showing up over and over. That's what you do if you want better, longer relationships.

There are battles you cannot win with "the right attitude." And, not everything happens for a reason.

Sometimes you won't be happy. Sometimes everything will suck. It's OK to not be OK.

Your purpose is not something you find.

Never ask what the meaning of life is. The meaning of life is up to you.

The more you love yourself, the more comfortable you are alone, the easier everything else will become.

The more open you are, the less vulnerable.

Feelings are fleeting, and they are not commands. They are not even suggestions.

Thoughts are just thoughts.

Your perception is not reality.

Your opinion is not a fact.

Your expectations will sink your relationships.

Your assumptions will lead you astray.

You will have less of whatever you chase.

Waiting is a form of inaction. It's not a virtue.

Action begets motivation — not the other way around.

Disappointment is an inside job. So is happiness.

Blame is a decoy. You do things to yourself.

You will betray yourself. Love yourself anyway.

A white lie is a lie.

Everything changes.

Nothing is yours to keep. Nothing. There are no exceptions.

You are going to die. So is everyone you love.

The time when you have it all figured out does not exist. I don't know what I'm doing. I forget everything I learn. It's why I write it down.

Are Humans Lonely, Afraid and Bigoted?

Yes. Heck yes. Humans are indeed lonely, afraid and bigoted.

We are also heroic, connected, committed and true.

We are empty, forsaken, bewildering, dashing, desperate and filled with joy.

Exalted and mourning, lost and found, present and wandering, reckless, hopeless, cowards and brave. So brave. Pure courage: determined and dauntless.

Whatever you hear about humans — anything — remember the opposite is in equal measure, just as true.

This is what makes us splendid, dazzling; and, yeah, miserable, drab and unaware.

What's Holding You Back?

My brain is super full of herself.

She will do anything to defend all the things she believes.

A lot of what she believes is architected — specially designed — to hold me back.

It's not that she does not want me to succeed: it's that she wants me to always be safe.

To move past all the things that limit me, I have to disbelieve — defy — my own thinking. I have to, in a very real sense, wrestle with my brain.

As I do this, I learn to move past my thoughts onto a wide open space where I can catch glimpses of everything I can be.

It's a tough, hard world out there, despite which what stands between me and all I can be is for the most part me.

Who Bores You?

My ego exhausts me.

Here is what she sounds like:

What will everyone think of me?

What will people say?

Life is so unfair.

I made a mistake.

I made the wrong decision.

I can't believe he betrayed me.

I feel like nobody wants me.

I feel like nobody sees me.

Why does nobody understand me?

Why don't people choose me?

I feel like I don't matter.

I feel no one makes an effort for me.

I feel like he doesn't love me the way I want him to.

I feel like no one can be trusted.

Why is nothing working for me?

I am not enough.

She is better than me.

That thing is holding me back.

When I am criticized, the criticism is true.

I need to be better.

I need to try harder.

I need to earn the love of others.

So, yeah. Me. I bore me.

If You Are Not on Instagram, Do You Exist?

Do you want to hear something wonderful and disturbing and beautiful?

We don't know if we exist.

Wondering — pondering — if we do or don't is a very deep, very human thing to do.

The French philosopher Descartes proposed that *"we could not doubt our existence while doubting"* meaning that the fact that he doubted was proof that he existed. (*"Cogito ergo sum."*)

To put it in other words, if I'm sitting here wondering if I exist it must mean I do, because otherwise who is doing all this wondering?

I can say with authority that I wondered about my existence before Instagram's existence.

This is how I conclude that even if I was not on Instagram, I would exist.

Still, I am on Instagram. You know — just in case.

Can a Short-Tempered Person Be Happy?

Being short-tempered implies there is hardly a sliver of distance between what I think and feel and how I act.

This makes me highly reactive.

Reacting to all my thoughts and all my feelings has me in a constant state of reaction. Reaction. Reaction.

This is exhausting.

My reactions might be shutting down or not talking to others. Being defensive. Judging. Being aggressive.

All this makes me unsteady, erratic, volatile and quite unstable — makes others feel like they never know what to expect from me or my behavior.

To separate myself from my thoughts and feelings, I need to separate myself from them. I need to look at them: become a witness. Then, I need to question them.

Wow. This has made me angry. Why? What was it about this that made me feel trapped? What do I need? How can I best represent myself?

To me, there is deep happiness and peace in giving myself a break from being in a constant state of reacting to the storm of all the feelings inside of me. My wrath is usually related to feeling like no one can hear me or see me, and this is how I learn to hear and see myself.

How Can I Be Myself?

In my experience, this is less about being and more about exploring.

By this I mean it's a process, takes a long time, and has an evolution. (Meaning, it changes. You change.)

I ask myself what I want and then am curious about what happens when I get it. (Hmmm. I thought that was what I wanted but I guess not.)

I look for the things that I like and that are important to me.

I identify the things that are not me and do less of them. (I understand cars are sexy but honestly. I could not possibly care any less what you drive.)

Sometimes this is hard because a lot of other people like certain things, so not liking them makes me feel like there is something wrong with me. (Nope. I'm OK.)

A few examples I can think of:

Being at a party and arriving home late and wondering why I feel so exhausted and so hollowed out. (I don't like parties.)

Being alone for many days at a time and wondering why I feel so empty. (I love social interaction — I just need time to recharge.)

98

Writing and feeling electric, plugged into the whole universe. (Yep. This is it. This is what I want more, more, more of.)

Falling in love and getting married and feeling like that ring felt like a noose. Marriage is wonderful. Just because something is wonderful doesn't mean it's right for me.

So that's what you do — step. Review. Step. How do I feel? Step. What do I need? Step. Why does this feel awful when it's supposed to feel wonderful?

This exploration is not tiresome or stressful. (Well, OK. Sometimes it is.) But mostly it's the delightful discovery of this interesting person that you are. You get to know her, and slowly, astonishingly, you become yourself.

What PMS Feels Like

Sometimes I feel anxious or worried about something that doesn't actually take place. Afterwards I realize that all that suffering happened due to an incident that only existed in my head. It was painful and I did it to myself.

I want to learn how to regulate my worry and anxiety to make life easier on me, but then I go and I do it again. And again. Why?

The reason is because my worry and stress sound like me. They sound like my voice of reason. Like reality. It's very, very difficult to distinguish this fake angst and anguish and dread from a real threat because all these very clear, very real sensations are coming from inside me.

This is exactly what I feel when I feel hormonal. Life becomes overwhelming. Others become irritating. People experience trouble understanding me, and so naturally I feel misunderstood and also I'm hungry and don't know why people who once loved me no longer do. So I cry. I cry if someone asks me to, say, set the table, because can't you see? Everything is falling apart. Nothing is in its place, so how can you be thinking about table setting at a time like this?

Of course this is something I want to regulate. I will suffer less if I can look at my sense that everything is overwhelming right in the face and say *"You don't exist. You are not real. You are*

hormones, and everything will look better a few days from now."
But it's very, very hard. Because, hormones sound exactly like me. They sound like I can finally see things as they really are.

To better understand someone going through PMS, think about how it felt when you were in the grip of anxiety. About the last time you worried about something that never took place. Think about the last time you were angry and how anger felt just like it feels when you can finally see things clearly.

How Can You Free Yourself?

All my life I thought the answers to everything were in my thoughts. *"Dushka, think"* was one of the central commands I was raised with.

The older I get the more I learn that the answers are actually in my body. My thoughts shift, they swirl, they think one thing, then another.

The answers I seek (what do you want? What do you need? Where can I find happiness?) and way to freedom are not in my thoughts. They are in my body.

Top of Your Game

My ego loves to spin stories. This is what she does all day long.

"You are no longer at the top of your game" is the artist formerly known as *"you are not enough."*

"You are too old to do that" is the new *"you are too young to do that."*

I quietly observe my ego's stories.

"Don't even write that. No one is going to read it."

"What's the point of meditating, if you're not doing it right?"

"Ugh. I have no idea what I'm doing."

"Thank you" I say to my ego, all fluster and restlessness and curly hair. *"Thank you for trying to keep us safe. But you know what we're going to do? We're going to go ahead and do that thing you are trying to discourage us from doing."*

Because, there is no "game". There is no "top." All I have is what I can do, and I happen to believe right to my core that it's enough.

I believe that whatever you can do is enough too.

Why Do People Need to Give Advice?

If you are single, people feel the need to give you advice on how to get out of your unfortunate situation. As if being single was a tragic state of suspension. As if you didn't exist without another.

If you are dating, people dispense dating advice.

If you have been dating for a while, people begin to ask when you are finally getting married.

If you are married, people ask when you will have children, or why you haven't had them.

If you get pregnant — whoa. Ask any pregnant woman the wave of advice they get hit with. And, the kind of mother you should be. Why staying at home with your kids will ruin them. Why going back to work will ruin them. How you should raise them.

Advice is an act of the ego disguised as generosity or concern. It carries within the assumption that the person giving it knows better than you. Better than you, about your own life.

Also, advice is projection. I am not really giving you advice. I am judging myself. Doubting myself. I am trying to teach you what I need to learn.

How Can I Change the Fact That I Chase What I Don't Have?

What you are describing is a powerful insight and the opposite of gratitude.

A practice of gratitude is hard but if you keep at it, it shifts into your brain focusing on what you do have, and how lucky you are to have it.

A practice of gratitude requires that you show up for it, that you keep returning to it, to get your brain used to identifying it.

Here are a few exercises to try:

Get together with a small group of friends and go around with each one saying what they are grateful for. Each participant gets three turns. (So you go around the circle three times.)

Get together with one friend and say *"tell me in two minutes ten things you are grateful for."* Then it's your turn.

A gratitude notebook. Before going to bed write down a list of ten things that happened on that day that you are grateful for.

I am excited for anyone who gives these exercises a try. I can't wait for you to show yourself how incredibly fortunate you already are.

How Can I Read More if I Dread It?

When I demand too much of myself and this accomplishes the opposite of what I want, I drastically reduce my expectations.

Instead of dreading reading, for example, I get a really fun, simple book.

I tell myself there is no point in me reading it other than my own entertainment — it doesn't matter how quickly I do so, how much I understand or in how much time.

As soon as the pressure is off, I find reading it a delight. I remember the simple story and recommend it to others.

This exercises my reading muscle and typically results in me picking up something a bit harder.

To be more effective, it never pays off to beat myself up. I react much better if I'm treated with love, in particular from myself.

How Do I Know if I Am an Introvert?

An introvert is defined as someone who is drained by social interaction and who needs to be alone to recharge.

It has nothing to do with being shy, reserved or socially anxious.

It does not mean I don't like people.

Here are some things I do that indicate I'm an introvert:

I rarely pick up my phone. If it rings I look at it in horror, even if I want to talk to the person who is calling.

I have an aversion to small talk and take great measures to avoid it.

I would do anything to avoid a crowd: I decline invitations to parties, festivals and concerts.

I really, really like my friends. I don't hang out with people just to hang out with someone.

When I hang out with good friends I leave early.

If someone cancels our plans to be together I feel relief. I rejoice, even if I love them.

I plan my day so I have a lot of time to myself and really enjoy being alone.

I try not to put myself in situations where I am trapped and cannot recharge. I would never travel with a group of friends or have a sleepover; and it is rare for me to invite someone over to my house. I need to know them well enough to know that I can ask them to leave without insulting them.

What Things Should I Never Do?

Believe the voice inside you that whispers any version of *"you are not enough."* It can sound like *"you are too young"* or *"you are too old"* or *"your best work is behind you."*

Compromise who you are in an effort to get someone to love you.

Crave validation from people who don't lead a life you'd want for yourself.

Look for happiness in events that are supposed to be milestones. (After a wedding, for example, you will still have to contend with you.)

Berate yourself.

Do something that doesn't really interest you because it's what "everybody" does.

Say "I'm fine" when you are not.

Feel like you need to read someone else's mind.

Feel guilty about setting boundaries.

Apologize when you say no.

Explain or justify your choices.

Stay past the point when you'd rather just go home.

What Is Broken Inside of You?

I believe we all have something invincible inside of us. It's not that we don't break — it's that we recover. We bounce back. We are emotional superheroes.

I know. Sometimes I feel hopeless too.

But, feelings are temporary.

I hold the following as true:

I have resources. This can mean many different things: access to doctors, access to a massage therapist, access to a yoga class, support from a stranger.

The sense that I am alone in this is an illusion.

I can nurture relationships that are loving and supportive. This is like moving through life with a large security net under me always.

I can be deliberate with the single thing I can control: my attention. I give it to beauty and light and truth. I take it away from anything that makes me feel crappy.

I spend time alone. This grants me the space I need to sort myself out. To think less. To "survive" less, struggle less, react less. Observe more. Feel more.

I keep reminding myself that where things are at is in my body and in my breath — not in my thoughts. My thoughts freak out and lie. They need to be observed, questioned and soothed.

I practice setting boundaries and saying no, which is an essential step in treating myself with respect.

Despite how it might feel sometimes, there is nothing broken inside of me, and when there is, I can mend it.

The same is true for you.

Have You Ever Felt Lonely?

Let me tell you a few things every human feels at one point or another:

My life has no meaning.

I have no purpose.

I am worthless.

I feel trapped.

I want to escape this life and start over somewhere far away.

I am sad.

I am anxious.

I feel grief.

I feel shame.

I don't understand what's wrong with me.

Everyone else is better than me.

I want what someone else has (envy).

Someone will take away something that is mine (jealousy).

People think I'm good at X and instead I am an impostor.

Someone else can save me.

I can fix someone else.

I am lonely.

The question is this: if we all feel this way, is it true that we are alone?

Life Lessons I Learned the Hard Way

My thoughts lie to me.

My feelings are temporary.

My feelings need to be felt.

Discipline, far from punishing, is the highest, truest manifestation of self-love.

Doing only what I'm good at means I never learn anything new.

Familiar does not always equal good.

Love feels safe and is not supposed to hurt.

I don't have to be useful to deserve love.

It's necessary to put myself first.

Boundaries are not selfish.

Disappointing others is inevitable.

Most of what hurts does not exist.

Most of what I worry about will not happen.

I am not responsible for managing the emotions or the perceptions of others.

I cannot control, fix, save or improve someone else.

No one can control, fix, save or improve me.

The only person who can help me is me.

A trigger is something to work through and not something to run from.

People who deny my experience are toxic.

How other people behave does not define me. It defines them.

Deep breaths have the power to alter my mental space.

When someone talks about another they are talking about themselves.

Giving advice is an act of ego.

Silence is the antidote to feeling lost.

The more I tell myself I am too busy for yoga the more I need yoga.

How Can I Focus on Myself?

First, forever abandon the notion that self-care is selfish. This belief is destructive and ensures you end up isolated, resentful and depleted. This belief is why people burn out.

Ask yourself what you need. A bath? An orange? A divorce? What you need is hard to determine but the more you find time alone and the more patient you are with yourself the clearer the answer will become.

Consider learning how to meditate. It's the most glorious gift you will ever present yourself with: permission to set it all aside to make room for your breath.

Treat yourself like you would someone you love. With compassion, with generosity, with tolerance. *It's ok, Dushka. I've got you.*

Learn to say no. Boundaries are integral to this effort and saying no is a good start.

Make choices for you. If someone else tells you you are thinking of you instead of them, if they want to push you in a way that is to your detriment and their benefit — well, think about that.

Watch what you eat. Give yourself nutritious food. Make sure you are sleeping well. Learn how to breathe. Deep breaths

116

change your life — they tell your body you are OK. Eventually breathing deeply pulls you out of feeling like life is something you have to survive.

Move. Exercise. Find something you like — or more than one thing — so it's less of an effort and more of a respite, a vacation, a reward.

Find pleasure. I will give you a tip: it's in your senses. Things that feel good, taste good, sound good. Beauty is primal and necessary. Surround yourself with it.

The meaning of life is in connection. Identify people who inspire you and build you up and keep them near you.

Create something. A book. A garden. A dish. A company. We are creators.

There is solace and peace in repetition. Find your habits. Find your rituals. Find your ceremony. Serve yourself coffee every morning in silence. Pour it into a beautiful handmade cup. Write down things you are grateful for as you sip. Do it again, and again, and again.

Finally, these are not changes you make. This is a new life you step into. It's a practice, and you come back to it over and over. Did you say yes when you wanted to say no? It's ok. It's ok. You will try again tomorrow.

The Most Essential Human Need

Setting aside the most obvious things, such as food and water and being safe, the most essential human needs are:

Purpose (or meaning).

Connection.

Validation (being seen, understood — not from ego, but from identity).

Belonging.

The sense that you are leaving something behind (legacy).

Is the life you lead devoid of any of these things? Without them, it's natural to feel unmoored and lost, since these are the things that define our humanity.

What Is the Best Way to Evolve?

The first is how I use my time. Do I feel I have none? Am I very busy, with nothing to show for it? How can what I do have more meaning? How can it incrementally amount to something important to me?

Forget about big, sweeping changes. Look at the small things. What I do every day results in something. What is it that I am doing every day?

The second is how I connect to others. Does it feel like learning, like an opening, like inspiration, like wow? Or does it feel like gossiping and complaining is what connects me to others? The second is not real communication — it's like walking on a treadmill, expending energy but going nowhere.

The third is my regard for my past. Am I angry, bitter, full of resentment, remorse? Do I wish I could change it, take it back? Or can I see it as the reason why I am who I am today? Can I regard it with gratitude for what it has given me?

The fourth is how I treat myself. Do I take care of myself, make choices that are nourishing in every sense of the word? How does what I do to myself make me feel, and how can I make myself feel loved, taken care of, safe? How can I give to myself what I once expected others to give me?

Finally, I look at my thoughts. Are they indivisible from me or can I create space between me and them? If they tell me I am not enough, am I in a place where I can defy them? *I see you, thought, and I don't believe you.*

What Thoughts Do You Have While Meditating?

I need to focus on my breath. Inhale, exhale. After this I need to remember to go pick up the — wait, no. Back to my breath.

What a gift. For the next ten minutes I don't have to do anything, figure anything out — wait, no. Back to my breath.

I can't wait for this thing that hurts to stop hurting. My life will be better, I think, when — wait, no. Back to my breath.

Can I even do this? Am I just sitting here wasting my time, eyes closed, pretending to "meditate"? This is not helping. I'm doing it wrong.

But meditating isn't not thinking. It's the awareness that I'm thinking. And I'm aware that I'm thinking! Maybe I'm doing it — wait, no. Back to the breath.

When Do We Achieve Emotional Maturity?

If no one has told you, I am going to.

The magical location that you speak of does not exist.

No one ever reaches "emotional maturity." Emotional maturity, perhaps like happiness, is ever-elusive, a mythological thing that you sometimes brush up against but mostly just strive for.

I remember the day my nephew understood how it was less painful to assume responsibility (I did that) than to cast blame (someone else did this to me). He was seven.

I remember the tantrum one of my mother's friends threw because she was taking personally something that was actually not related to her. She was 76.

We strive. We swing back and forth, back and forth. We assume others have landed upon a formula that we scramble to find.

The truth is this: we are all babies. We are pure ego. We do our best.

Ataraxia

There's a story my yoga teacher likes to tell.

It's about a farmer. He has a horse, and one morning the horse gallops off into the hills.

What bad luck, his neighbors say. *You relied on that horse for everything.*

Good luck, bad luck, the man responds. *Who knows?*

The horse trots back the next day, flanked by a pack of wild horses. The farmer manages to corral them.

What amazing luck! his neighbors say.

Good luck, bad luck, the man responds. *Who knows?*

The next day his son tries to ride one of the wild horses. He falls and breaks his leg.

Oh, no, say the neighbors. *What terrible luck.*

Good luck, bad luck, the man responds. *Who knows?*

Soon, the king calls for all able bodied men to fight a war they are unlikely to return from. With his injury, the son cannot go.

The point of the story is ataraxia — the practice of remaining unperturbed. To exercise regarding things with equanimity. To accept. To remember: this too shall pass.

Rudyard Kipling included this concept in his staggeringly comprehensive poem "If" — *"If you can meet with Triumph and Disaster and treat those two impostors just the same."*

Equanimity is not about indifference, which is a life-extinguishing absence of concern. It's instead about internal evenness, emotional smoothness, intellectual stability. It's the freedom from any previous mental construct.

If You Want to Be Alone

It feels like your head is full of noise and rattle and suddenly the world quiets down.

It feels like everything is pulling at you, yanking at you, and you break free and step out and it lessens, then stops.

It feels like you are tired, so tired, and have been standing for so long and you spot a safe, clean place where you can lie down.

You set your head on a pillow. You put your feet up.

It feels like it's all a jumble, clutter, disarray, and you clean it out, wipe the counters.

It feels like bad weather, like a storm, and you open a door and step inside a dry room.

It has polished wood floors and a crackling fireplace and a library and the only person here is you.

Should You Stop Caring So Much?

Imagine an ocean.

You are swimming, swimming in rough, choppy water. It's turbulent in there, unstable and tempestuous and blustery, and you simply don't know how you can stay alive for much longer.

Now imagine you have a small, sturdy boat. You're in the storm for sure, invested, involved, impassioned, but you're also safe and dry.

I don't think it's a matter of not caring. I think it's about learning how not to let it pull you under.

How Do You Deal With Grief?

Here are some things that helped me:

Reminding myself that on bad days all I need to do is hold on.

Slowing down. Grief alters my notion of time — it feels like the world is moving at warp speed and I am caught moving through molasses. Slowing down in every possible way, including demanding less of myself, helps.

Surrounding myself with people who feel similarly. For example, the first week after my father died I spent every minute of the day with my siblings. It was the saddest, darkest time, but I remember it with so much love.

Giving myself space to grieve. I cried in public places, told people at work that I would cry in meetings, and in general didn't let anyone tell me to *"cheer up"* or to *"not be sad"*. Grief needs room. Give it room.

Letting my body exercise its own wisdom. If I was not hungry I would not eat, if I felt ravenous I would eat more. I would sleep if I felt tired (grief is exhausting) and I cried, a lot. After bouts of crying I always felt a bit better.

I am convinced crying is cleansing and healthy so I try not to hold it back. I've practiced crying with total abandon. I think it alarms people, this absolute surrender to sobbing, but it always brings relief.

Breathe. Any activity that helps me regulate my breath, like guided meditation or yoga, helps me a lot. Do not underestimate the power of deep breaths. While I'm trying to breathe I unfailingly have thoughts about how ridiculous it is, but afterwards I am stunned by the difference it makes.

Touch. Touch helps me a lot. I hug people. I ask friends to hold me. I get massages. I find touch incredibly therapeutic and comforting.

I tried grief counseling and felt very impatient with it. I felt it encroached on my space. I tried group therapy, where we talked about our loss in a small circle, and found it a lot more helpful. Different things work for different people. Explore.

One of the things I discovered was that I didn't want to feel better. At first, grief was a form of company — like, I don't have you anymore, but I have this, which is the closest I can come. Later, it felt like feeling better was a form of betrayal or abandonment of the person I had lost. I needed to articulate this and come to terms with it in order to let it go.

For the most part, the best remedy to grief is time. I lost my father five years ago and it hurts differently. I can't say it hurts less or that it gets better, but it shifts in a way that becomes more tolerable, at least most of the time.

Finally, know that grief will change you. Things will never be the same. At first I found this sad, and now I am grateful for the way it inexorably altered the course of everything.

Can You Forget What Hurt You?

I hope never to forget what hurt me.

I'd get burned on the same frying pan again and again, get pricked by a needle again and again, experience again and again the shard of glass that sliced right through the skin on the palm of my hand.

I hope not to forget the times I felt heartbroken. It's how I learned how important boundaries were, how not to compromise myself.

I remember what hurts me because slowly, slowly I learn. I learn what to stay away from, or when to try again.

Because, some things are worth the getting hurt.

But, not because I'm willing doesn't mean I don't remember.

How Can I Learn Not to Cry?

Your body is very, very wise. She has devised an integrated, natural purifier, an efficient way to eliminate toxins, to quickly release stress, like a well-designed valve sitting at the top of a pressure cooker. Crying is cathartic, calming, and very helpful in regulating your emotions. It actually improves your mood and even helps reduce pain.

Deciding not to cry is bending to a social construct. We determine to hold back the very mechanism designed to soothe and encourage us in order to uphold what we believe others demand from us.

As I've gotten older, I practice not holding back when I feel like crying. It's hard — it scares me and even makes me feel a measure of shame. But, crying feels cleansing, restoring, and even absolving — I always feel better after a good cry.

Maybe crying with abandon in front of others alarms them, but I've decided my health comes before whatever another person might think of me for having a healthy, expressive, normal physiological response to frustration, to anger, to pain.

Galaxy

I was born perfect.

This is because as a newborn I had not yet heard *"that's not 'normal'"* or *"let me tell you who you need to be"* or *"what are people going to think"* or even *"if you're not happy you're doing life wrong."*

In time, these mostly well-intentioned outside voices penetrated my cellular walls and became what I now mistakenly identify as a relentless, critical inner voice.

From here, I developed habits that are not who I am. They are more like crusts of something painful and foreign originally architected to protect me: anxiety, the illusion of limitation and impossibility, a sense of loneliness or that I am lost, a belief that I am weak and that life is both difficult and meaningless.

This is why spending time with yourself is so important. So you can listen.

There is a whole world inside you, a galaxy to discover, where you go reverse and unlearn all the things that are not true.

Things are not as you think they are. For example: There is nothing wrong with you. There is no such thing as "normal." No one is happy all the time. Everyone struggles. Your weaknesses are your strengths. What challenges you is designed for you to grow and is not misfortune but a gift.

131

There are no guides or gurus. No one outside you has what you will find if you go inside: answers, peace, purpose, connection.

You were born perfect. Go find her.

Longing

One of the most complicated feelings I feel is longing.

It's complicated because it feels so pure and so true. A white hot bolt that shoots through me and cinders at the back of my heart.

It's complicated because it's always in disguise. It feels like I long for one thing when really I long for another. It feels like I long for your body when really what I long for is the time I believed someone else could take care of me.

Longing feels like a primal command. Go get this thing you long for. It's taken me a long time to learn that longing is just a feeling and like any feeling it's mere sensation — not direction or imperative or even a suggestion.

I don't need that. I long for it — and those two are not the same.

Social Media

Let me tell you the most important thing I've learned about social media and how people use it: it is not an indicator of how people feel.

Sometimes I have feelings for someone and never look at their posts. Sometimes I feel nothing and am curious about how they think or what they say.

There is no correlation between what I do and click on and say on social media and how I feel about someone and there is no correlation between what someone else does and clicks on and says on social media and how they feel about me and if I think there is I will torture myself checking and checking and attempting to figure it out.

I do myself a favor and step back and close the darn app for a few days or weeks. Then, if I want to know if someone has feelings for me, I walk over to them and ask them in real life.

Social media can be fun or it can be brutal. I try not to make it brutal.

Do You Find It Easy to Say "No"?

I find it easy to say no when it comes to something I don't want to do. (For example, turning down an invitation to a birthday party.)

I find it very difficult not to volunteer a yes when the yes is none of my business. I always want to help. I always feel that doing something about what another person is struggling with is my responsibility.

This is not a generous trait. It's invasive, disguised as generous, and it takes constant work for me to hold back.

I am perpetually whispering to myself *"you don't need to fix or help or assist others. They don't need you to swoop in and meddle. What they need is for you to grant them the space to figure it out on their own."*

We all have our battles.

Anxiety Management

Four things help me manage my anxiety—

Questioning it. *Hello, anxiety. What are you trying to tell me? Not at an obvious level (run!) but at a deeper level. What is it, Dushka, that you are really trying to run from? What is it that's causing you to feel you're in imminent danger?*

Self-love. *Anxiety, I am not going to meet you with shame or exasperation. I am not going to say you shouldn't be feeling what you're feeling. I will instead snuggle you and soothe you and love you and serve you tea. I have a soft, heavy blanket waiting for you. Of course you're scared. Let's take deep breaths. Deep, deep breaths.*

Time alone. This space, this silence, is where you can hear yourself. *Tell me. What's going on? Whatever it is, I've got you. I've got us both. We are safe.*

Gratitude. *Thank you anxiety for the things you alert me to. How would I be able to be in touch with myself if it wasn't for your clear call, like a flare in the dark? Thank you for existing. I keep you safe, and you know what? You do the same for me.*

Boundaries/Comfort Zone

Breaking your boundaries feels like self-betrayal, like you have turned your back on yourself. It fills you with resentment — which is anger at yourself, disguised as anger towards another person.

Getting out of your comfort zone feels frightening but there is a sense of expansion, of breaking out of that place holding you in. You know that on the other side, instead of bitterness and displeasure, what you will feel is free.

Destined to Be a Failure

I am familiar with that voice — it's my anxiety and it sounds like me, or like an oracle.

I interrupt it.

What if, anxiety? What if things work out? What if I set goals and exceed them? What if I am met with unexpected serendipity?

What if I am a success?

Do you know what, anxiety? You are relentless, and persistent, but you can't tell the future. You don't know. You have no idea! Ha!

This means that my future scenarios are just as plausible as yours.

What Snapped You Out of Your Slump?

A snap. A strike. A crack, like a whip.

Love at first sight. The moment. The break. The catch.

We love the mythology of the instant everything changed. And sometimes life does that, but most of the time things take place at a low, slow simmer. Most of the time there is no sparkle, no puff, but rather an indistinguishable moment that layers on top of another on top of another.

More often than not things shift slowly, life rolls at the pace of a glacier, and then you look back and are incredulous to realize how far you've come.

I'm telling you this because there is a metamorphosis taking place inside you even when it feels you are idle. Just because you haven't felt a kaboom doesn't mean nothing is happening.

Whenever I'm in a slump I am already moving past it, because nothing, nothing is ever static, even when it feels that way.

What About Social Interaction Depletes You?

When I'm home alone I wear soft garments and fuzzy socks and dedicate my time to the pursuit of things that interest me. To go out into the world and interact with others requires that I put on real clothes.

While in part I mean this literally, it's also a metaphor for a layer I have to put on to make myself socially acceptable.

I carry with me a sensation that a bit of what I'm presenting is real, natural and comfortable, but not as real, natural and comfortable as I am when I am alone.

I don't mean artifice. I don't mean I wear a mask, because I don't. I don't mean I fake a persona, because I don't think I could. I'm referring to a level of ordinary, expected social adornment, a veneer of civility that I consider lovely, necessary and most definitely an effort.

When I'm "being social" I am definitely "being me", really, really me, but I'm being "on" me. This alertness is not unpleasant — I actually quite like it — but represents to me an expenditure of energy.

When I talk to others I take on the responsibility of keeping an interesting conversation going. It feels like I'm swimming. I can't just nod and float. I keep moving my arms and legs vigorously so

140

my head can remain above water. Metaphor aside, I love swimming. It's just tiring.

I have to listen — remain engaged, interested — and then say something in response. I find both these things first insistent, then demanding, later cloying of my attention and brain function.

As I become more tired, my ability to manage input is compromised. I feel overstimulated. Threads of conversation that were once tidy begin to seem disjointed, tangled. Following becomes harder, in particular if I am not interested (which is the case with small talk).

I become a stranger, an outsider in a conversation that I created.

Then there is noise management. If I am talking to you and we have to scream over background music or background banging or background chatter, if I have to hear you but someone near you is having a conversation with someone else that I can also hear, I feel my brain short circuit. It blows a fuse. It's a horrible feeling. Aside from the physical sensation of the energy leaking out my ears I feel a sense of anger like *what the hell Dushka what on earth are we doing here.*

Then, I am overwhelmed by the feeling that I am sacrificing something precious in exchange for this. I am allowing myself to be pulled away from something somewhere else that is truer to me.

I want to go home. I want to be in my house with my things and my words. I want to go be with me.

Why Does Grief Hurt?

My father died five years ago.

Five years ago, my life was completely different. Since the day of his death:

I walked away from a 20+ year career building agencies.

I got certified to teach yoga.

I stopped writing in lined notebooks that I stacked in drawers and began writing on social media platforms.

I took time off to write a book and have so far written eight.

I broke up after a seven year relationship.

I moved out of my apartment.

I got a new job.

I drastically changed my role at said job.

I found an airy apartment, designed for one person, and bought it.

These changes had an inevitable impact on the people I frequent and how I spend my time.

It feels like there is a wide current of grief winding through me that is carving out a new inner landscape.

So many things that have happened to me I did not consider plausible even a short time ago.

Grief hurts because it kills you.

How Do I Identify My Ego?

My ego is persuasive, high-strung, kinetic, hyperactive and indivisible from me. She wants me to believe I'm the center of the world, and wants to keep me safe.

She loves drama (closed, fabricated, theatrical) and despises risk (open, adventurous, uncomfortable).

Whenever I judge other people, the things they do, the choices they make, that's my ego trying to reassure me that whatever I am doing is much better.

Whenever I compare myself to others or insist on being right or get defensive or cast blame, that's her. Being perceived as fallible makes her frantic.

Whenever I repeat old patterns, that's her pulling me back in — she identifies "familiar" with safe so wants me to relive the same painful dynamic. She already knows it hurts but in its repetition has confirmed it's unlikely to kill me.

Whenever I'm more agitated about the story (not real) than about the fact (real), that's her. (Have you ever gotten angry over an argument that has only taken place in your head?)

Whenever I focus on approval or validation more than on what I want, that's her.

144

The way she relates to others is taking everything personally (because, it's all about her). This sounds like "you would if you loved me" or "you need to make me happy" or "I can fix you" or "please don't leave me". (*But Dushka. What if in leaving, you are being set free?*)

She believes that she needs to do something — be useful, be good — to deserve love.

The way she relates to creation or creativity or anything I do that might be beautiful is to sound like "I have no idea what I'm doing" or "I'm not doing it right" or "I failed". (*But, Dushka. What if you learned?*)

What you need to do with the ego is observe her. *Oh, wow. There you go again.* Question her. *Really? Is this story you just spun really truly true?* And soothe her. *Oh, my sweet. it's OK. We're going to be ok.*

Nothing to Be Grateful For

There is a natural force that attracts particles, objects
and bodies. Without it we'd lose the moon. Earth itself
would disappear.

Everything around you, no longer held together by everything
around it, would begin to lift.

Air — and with it the oxygen you need to breathe — would
dissipate into space.

The same would happen to water — rivers, lakes, oceans and all
the life they hold.

This is a good place to start.

Thank you. Thank you for gravity.

Not Worth It

Complaining.

Keeping secrets.

Believing everything you think.

Overthinking.

Worrying.

Blame.

Grudges.

Trying to control another person or expecting to change them.

Trying to save or fix another.

Thinking that anything outside of you can fix or save you.

Regarding yourself as a victim.

Regarding everyone with suspicion.

Comparing yourself to others.

Compromising your boundaries to please someone.

Looking at your phone when people right in front of you need your attention.

Staying in an unhealthy relationship because you're afraid to be alone.

Breaking any promise you make to yourself. Nothing is worth more than teaching yourself you can trust you.

Anything you do because "it's cool" and not because you want to.

Justifying yourself.

Judging others.

Staying at a job that makes you unhappy or where you are not learning anything new.

If you look at social media and it makes you feel like everyone's life is better than yours, your feed is not worth it. Adjust it so that what you are looking at inspires you, teaches you, uplifts you.

Check the Pool

I have a tendency to throw myself heart first into everything. It's full speed ahead, full tilt, all in.

This exuberance has given me everything in my life that is beautiful: love, deep relationships, meaningful friendships, a profession I feel passionate about, a clarity of expression.

This trait has also caused me every heartbreak, disenchantment, disillusion and the recurring sense that there is something wrong with me.

When I feel crushed I tell myself that I need to change. That I've had enough. That the solution, obviously, is to close my heart.

This is mostly because when I'm suffering I'm thinking *"here we go again"*. It exasperates me to realize that what shatters my heart has remained unchanged from when I was little. Isn't it time I eradicate this intensity?

I was talking about this with a friend: this choice that's high time I make. My heart — on, or off? *I can't,* I tell him. *I can't keep living like this. It's too painful.*

I think, he said, *it's less a matter of on or off and more a matter of being mindful. You can tell when you're on the brink of spilling over. You can tell — now. Now is when I dive headfirst without checking the pool. So, in that moment, don't dive. Stand on the rim, consider, edge back.*

149

It's not about change. It's about awareness. A whisper of your clear mind as you watch yourself playing out this thing you do.

Calibrate. Adjust as you go.

Is this easy? Of course not. Many times I know full well diving head first is unwise and I do it anyway because doing things with all my heart is such a high.

But maybe I can learn to stand on the edge, on the very tips of my toes, on this bouncy, bouncy trampoline, just a bit longer.

So that's what I will attempt to do. Be more present in the wild ride that is my own enthusiasm.

How Do I Find Who I Am?

I've felt lost many, many times throughout my life. I tried to find myself, in chronological order — in my parents, in my friends, in advice from strangers, in life-instruction books, in reaching out to the authors of these books.

In someone else's eyes, in someone else's arms, in someone else's soothing words, so many times wise and sensible but never quite right.

In getting married. In getting divorced.

I tried to find myself, believe it or not, by listening to people who did not lead a life I would want to lead. I have no idea how I ever thought this could possibly be helpful.

I know this sounds like a platitude but the answers were inside me all along.

How? How do I listen to them?

Here are some things that work for me:

Time alone and silence. The worse time alone feels, the more I need it.

More time in nature.

Getting out of my head and into my body. My thoughts think many contradicting things but my body is very clear — it feels light or heavy, it feels joy or dread, it feels safe or anxious. My body knows what my brain does not.

Writing. Getting up in the morning and writing how I feel, what I want, what I don't want. Sometimes when I don't know what to write I do other things, like sketching, drawing, even doodling.

I get clear on what to say no to and what to say yes to. I start creating boundaries and accept this probably means I will disappoint others.

I slowly — it's a process — stop doing all the things I should have never done in the first place. A few examples are assume responsibility for the emotions of others, doing things just to deserve being loved, trying to control others, taking things personally.

Little by little all these things will come together in a revolution. I begin to change, my relationships change, what I do with my day changes. I feel I am doing everything wrong. And one day, like the sky suddenly clearing, I feel found again.

What Do You Want Next?

Do you know what I want?

I want what I have right now.

I want to enjoy right now to the fullest.

I want to give myself the luxury of not worrying or fretting or designing or planning or dreaming up what comes next.

I want to live in the beautiful, surprising, sometimes painful right now, without expectation or anxiety and without the sensation that I am just on my way to another place, or that there is something pending, someone to get to, something missing or something yet to find or complete or improve upon.

Otherwise I will miss it, you see.

And one day soon I will have whatever and look back at today and wonder why on earth I didn't fully appreciate it.

Can You Detach From Your Emotions?

You can.

There is a healthy way, and an unhealthy way.

If you detach from your emotions by burying them, by ignoring them, by filling your life with distractions, by suffocating them, you are really ignoring and suffocating yourself. Emotions are a form of intelligence, and diminishing them means missing out on vital information about your world.

If you detach from your emotions by feeling them, by being a witness to them, by giving them space, by asking yourself why, by identifying what it is that makes you feel the way you do, then you are paying attention to yourself. You are listening, and practicing not getting tangled up. This is hard but slowly you learn that you are not your feelings, but rather the person who feels them.

The first option will disconnect you, from yourself and from everyone.

The second option is called self-awareness, and it is vital to happiness.

As an Introvert, How Do You Recharge?

I return to my empty apartment, sit on the couch with a snack and munch. Nothing to do. Nowhere to be. I'm just going to sit here in this semi-dark room with these crunchy delicacies.

I find my soft blanket, curl up somewhere warm and read.

I find solace and pleasure in texture so I pull out a worn sweatshirt, fuzzy socks, a fluffy pillow, a cozy outfit.

I love beauty treatments and things that smell good so I camp out in my bathroom with a hot oil hair treatment, a moisturizing face mask and lubricating foot cream. By the time I am ready to socialize I will be smooth, soft, sweet-smelling and lustrous.

I putter around my house. Setting things in order on the outside puts things in their place on the inside.

Nature helps me so very much. I go on a long hike or walk somewhere where I can see green or water. For periods of time I focus on my breath so that my thoughts can settle down.

I lie on the grass and look at the sky. I like watching clouds go by.

I exercise. When I am tired my brain doesn't want to do anything but I tell her that social interaction depletes my brain, not my body. I always feel better after exercise. When I feel like I'm too tired is when I needed it the most.

I window shop. I take a stroll and look at the displays. I loiter in a bookstore and sit in the couch on a sunny corner and flip through coffee table books. I read poems.

I go have a meal by myself. I love eating alone. I sit at a small table by a window and order something that will take a long time to eat, like boiling hot broth.

I grab a colorful towel and go sit in a park where I can people watch. I take notes.

I ride a bus. I like the movement and the vignettes that take place right in front of me. I later write bus stories.

I write. People ask me how I have time to write so much. How can I not? This is how I recover.

What Would You Like to Be Really Good At?

Breathing. Good, slow, deep, long breaths.

Regarding things with equanimity.

Creating space between anything and my reaction to it.

Getting used to being misunderstood.

Getting comfortable disappointing others.

Immediately recognizing when my ego has stepped in.

Stating my boundary and feeling no distress or difficulty holding strong when someone else doesn't approve.

Knowing that what I experienced is true without needing anyone to confirm its veracity.

Learning how to dance like Shakira.

What Skills Make Me a Better Human?

Self-love, which allows me to see things as they are, rather than defensively.

Selflessness, to always consider the thoughts and feelings of others rather than being under the illusion that anything revolves around me.

Generosity, to give, forgive and assume the best intentions in others.

Gratitude, to appreciate what I have rather than only have eyes for what I don't.

Non-judgment, to accept and understand both myself and other people.

Accountability as the antidote to blame.

Compassion, the ability to put myself in another person's shoes.

Courage, to face fear and be willing to make the right choice for myself even if I risk disappointing others.

Awkward

What is the big deal with "awkward"? Why oh why am I so afraid of it?

I have weighed myself down with a secret for years lest things get "awkward."

I have avoided repairing a valuable relationship because approaching the other person would have been awkward.

I have disposed of treasured people to circumvent the awkward stage of navigating whatever needed to be navigated — a transition, a breakup, a change.

Please, accept awkward. Let things be awkward. Embrace awkward.

Consider for a moment the cost (transitory awkwardness) versus what you stand to gain.

In the grand scheme of things, yeah, awkward is graceless and floundering and uncomfortable, but really, it's nothing compared with what is waiting on the other side.

What Should I Do if Someone Makes Me Angry?

When I am angry I wonder what on earth I can do to not be angry.

My anger disappoints me — I should be able to control, contain myself.

I have concluded that it's not possible to not be angry. Feelings cannot be extinguished at will. They are trying to tell me something.

What I can do is be aware of my anger so it doesn't become the boss of me.

Also, I can be compassionate with myself.

I am often disappointed by me, but you know what? If I am supportive and patient with others, I deserve to be supportive and patient with me.

If Life Is Hard, How Can You Make It Lighter?

You are not responsible for keeping the peace or making sure others are getting along.

You are not responsible for another person's expectations of you.

You are not responsible for what another person thinks about you.

You are not responsible for explaining yourself.

You are not responsible for how another person behaves.

You are not responsible for getting someone to love you (or even like you).

You are not responsible for helping, rescuing or saving anyone other than yourself.

You are not responsible for anyone's happiness (or their emotional state).

You are not responsible for how your boundaries make another person feel.

You are not responsible for being anyone another person wants you to be.

Why Is Acceptance So Hard?

Acceptance is about making contact with reality.

It's about letting go of how we imagined things to be but were clearly not.

It's the antidote to denial, to feeling constantly disappointed, to feeling regret.

You accept to make room for things to improve for you.

You accept as an integral part to suddenly understanding.

You accept when you open your eyes and decide at all costs to be honest with yourself.

Part of this process of accepting is to clearly see the role you played in whatever it is that is causing you pain.

How did I contribute to this situation I am in? Why did I choose to see things as they were not?

Acceptance is a form of release, a form of surrender — an acknowledgment that I do not have the power to change the way things are — kind of like forgiving yourself.

It's an important part of overcoming loss.

And

And.

And and and.

And, not or.

You don't have to choose.

Can You Describe the Road to Better Understanding and Loving Yourself?

I think it all begins when I feel completely lost. When I feel stuck, like the same things keep happening to me over and over.

I've tried everything, and still cannot seem to get the approval or love that I look for in others. I feel misunderstood and isolated.

I decide I've had enough.

I may not find what I need in others, but, I have me.

I need to learn how to stand by me — how to be the one who believes in me and supports me.

This means learning to make peace with the fact others might be disappointed or confused by my decisions.

I start to believe in my own self-worth, as something I inherently have rather than something I need to earn. My self worth is related just to being, not with doing or achieving.

I begin working towards giving more breath and life to what I think and what I want. This means I become more disciplined, more deliberate, more directed. Very slowly I see the results of the actions I take.

As I begin to see results, I see that I cannot impact other people's opinions of me. I have to remain focused on feeding my own opinion of me. This is how getting others to like me begins to become less important — in part because it would require that I distract myself from my own endeavors, and in part because I've learned I can't have an impact over what others feel or do.

I begin to care for myself, talk to myself and do things for myself that normally were reserved for others. I take me to the doctor, stop berating myself, become aware of my critical inner voice and begin to shift it towards being more loving and compassionate towards me.

I become increasingly comfortable with saying no — in particular to make room for all the things I want to do to honor myself.

My relationships begin to change. I lose people who seem unable to adjust to the fact that I am doing right by me.

I feel my life is tight, so tight. I need space to reconsider everything. I need to spend more time alone. I feel like nothing is what it seems.

I begin questioning my own thoughts. If my thoughts tell me I'm not enough, could it be my thoughts are lying to me? I begin to see how my feelings and my thoughts change the way I perceive things and are not necessarily true.

This interesting, sometimes painful, ultimately very beautiful trajectory is what it feels like to begin to learn to love myself.

Why Do We Feel Shame When It Comes to Mental Illness?

Because I want to be normal and this feels like I'm not.

Because I want to belong and this feels like I don't.

Because I don't want this to define me.

Because look at everyone else. Why is everyone else so happy? Why is everyone else OK?

Because clearly there is something wrong with me.

Because I feel like I'm broken.

Because I am so overwhelmed and shame is a form of paralysis.

Because I feel like I'm the only one who feels this way.

Because this is warping the way I see myself and now I feel powerless and small and tired. So tired.

Because no one is going to believe me.

Because feeling like I need help from someone else makes me feel weak.

Because I feel like this is my fault.

Because I feel like this is my fault.

Because I feel like this is my fault. I should be able to keep it together, and it feels like I can't.

How Can I Enjoy the Moment?

In my experience, what gets me out of the moment are my thoughts. They time travel — they go to the past or the future, whizzing around, distracting me from now.

What anchors me to now is my body. My senses. What is it that I am tasting? What am I hearing? What am I feeling? What do I see?

To learn to enjoy the moment I practice getting out of my head and into my body.

This is not action. It's practice. My thoughts are always thinking, carrying me somewhere else. *Come back, Dushka. Look. Look at what's right in front of us.*

Do You Have Healthy Boundaries?

My boundaries are pretty solid.

My boundaries are a catastrophe.

Let me explain.

In some ways my boundaries are very healthy. I have learned to say no. I can easily present my case. I step away from over-explaining something I don't really need to give explanations for. All these things used to be hard for me, but they are getting easier and easier.

In other ways my boundaries need so much work. I often feel responsible for the well-being of others, or how they feel. I have an urge to step in and try to fix whatever they are struggling with, which often ends up making me feel like I'm giving more than I should. This pattern leaves me feeling exhausted and often heartbroken, which basically means I exhaust myself, and break my own heart.

I work very hard at stepping away from the notion that I am valuable or lovable because I can help.

I don't have any tattoos but maybe I need one across my heart that reminds me I cannot save another. I can only save myself.

Is It Reasonable to Feel Hurt?

I have a friend who broke up with her boyfriend because she never saw him. They led parallel lives. *"If I was never with him,"* she asks me, *"why does this hurt so much?"*

I have another friend who just quit a job she loves for a fantastic opportunity. She is thrilled but also she is grieving. *"Why, Dushka? Why do I feel so sad if this is so fortunate?"*

Another friend lost his mom when he was a teenager. He's now in his mid-forties, and sometimes hides in the bathroom to cry. *"Why? Why do I still feel I am mourning after so many years?"*

And my question is this. Why? Why do we question our feelings? Why do we wonder if or even demand that they be "reasonable"?

Why do we need to be told that it's normal to be anxious, that there is loss in change even when it's good, that grief never really ends, that sometimes what we lose has to do with an aspiration, a broken dream, more than with what we actually had?

Why do we second-guess ourselves to the point that we need to ask permission to feel?

Noise

Let me share with you one of the most difficult, most useful things to understand to arrive at a better life.

Just because something works for everyone else doesn't mean it works for me.

Just because something doesn't work for anyone doesn't mean it won't work for me.

Each person needs to evaluate every single thing, to in effect start from scratch.

To disregard what works for others in order to discover what works for me.

What works for others is just noise — an impediment to understanding myself.

What I think is important and what others think is important does not matter. What matters is what works for you.

Find Ease

I know, I know.

You are running around doing so many things that only you can do, that require your attention.

Here is what I have to say to that.

Find ease.

A deep breath (or ten).

Sit in the sun.

Look out the window.

Sip tea.

Take a minute. Maybe (gasp) two.

Find ease.

All the things you need to do will be right there waiting for you.

A practice of ease is never wasted.

How Can You Tell if You're Developing Self-Awareness?

Symptoms of increased self-awareness:

I am clearer on how things make me feel. What makes me feel good? What makes me feel anxious? How does being around that person make me feel? How does doing this (nurtured, happy, healthy) or that (guilty, nervous) make me feel?

I used to feel and instantly react. Now, wait a minute. I feel anger. Why? Where is this coming from? Is the thought or series of thoughts that caused this anger real? Is this something I can breathe through? How can I best represent myself?

I am getting better at recognizing the voice of my ego. *Oh my god I am alone. What are people going to think of me? Why doesn't anyone understand me?* It's OK, ego. You are not alone. You never will be. I've got you.

I used to feel despair when someone misunderstood me or expressed disappointment. Now, I can watch that sensation. Can I make room in this tight, cavernous space? Can it be OK, to be misunderstood? Can I stand by the boundary I just created for myself?

Speaking of which, I am getting better at creating boundaries, at saying no to things so I have more space for myself — even when it feels scary or makes me feel like I'm being selfish.

I begin to do things I am scared of.

I have plans for myself and am following through on them.

I'm sad and very tired when I think of all the things I used to do that I couldn't see. My past behavior, my past suffering, my patterns.

Spending time alone used to make me feel restless and trapped. Now I love it, need it, crave it. Spending time alone feels wonderful but even when it doesn't I know it's solace: a steady place to go to sort myself out.

Things I Wish
Someone Had Told Me
About Relationships

Self-Love

Our relationship with ourselves sets the tone for every other relationship.

Without it, I try to be the person others want me to be, instead of the person I really am.

I believe every story my ego spins. That I'm not enough, that I'm stuck, that other people have better lives than mine.

I try to look for success and fulfillment outside of myself: a better house, a better car, a good husband. I will value myself when I get promoted. I will value myself when I have children.

If I look for people who can save me, fix me or approve of me I am likely to feel stuck or like I have no control over what happens to me. I feel overwhelmed and approach my relationships with despair.

If I don't know how to set boundaries I cannot respect the boundaries of another, since I don't understand them and interpret them as a form of rejection.

If I disregard my own feelings I am likely to show little empathy for the feelings of another.

If I don't take responsibility for myself, my decisions, my actions, I blame others for my circumstances and become increasingly powerless and bitter.

If I make commitments to myself and fail me, I am likely to fail others.

Self-love — asking myself what I can give to myself, questioning my own stories, assuming full responsibility for everything I am, following through on the promises I make to myself — will recast everything.

What's the Point of Getting Attached?

Life is weird. It's so weird. I could write a whole paragraph of massively contradicting things about life and they would all be true: dazzling and terrible, cruel and breathtaking, magnanimous, benevolent and a total, unbelievable bitch.

Along the way you meet people and get attached.

This right here — this "getting attached" is the crux of the matter: it's where you learn and love and get hurt and grow and get taken out and recover and return to battle again and again.

This is what makes you want to spread out your arms like wings and break out in spontaneous song and dance — and this is what brings you to your knees.

To more directly answer the question, getting attached to people *is* the point.

Is Life Bullshit?

Keep the people you love close and determine to be interested in what they are interested in. Be all up in their business even if you have to apologize sometimes for overstepping. It's really difficult to love all clean and tidy. Or maybe it's just my love that's messy as hell.

Meet your friends' new significant others. Hold their newborn children and marvel at how fast they grow, like weeds, like puppies. Attend everyone's birthday parties. They will look back one day at their photo albums and see you there behind the lopsided cake year after year.

Spend time with the people that you love. There is no such thing as "quality time" or "power hours". Spend real time with those who matter to you. Yes, it's worth the plane ticket and the time out of the office.

Talking about people who matter to you, look at them. Make sure they feel seen. Never let anyone you love feel like you look through them or past them. Put your fucking phone down.

Take care of yourself as if you were precious (because you are). Move every day. Eat well. Read. I really don't care what.

Get out of your head and into your body. Make sure every single one of your senses gets to celebrate the fact that it exists. Taste something, maybe citrus. Touch something scratchy or coarse or feathery. Look at something that makes you squint or guffaw with its dazzle. Smell something that reminds you of when you used to be safe. Shhhhh — listen. Find the rhythm in people honking their car horns or blowing their noses. It's all symphony.

Find something that makes you feel and do it until it wrings you out. I've heard moderation is wise but it doesn't do very much for me.

Connect. Connection is the source of almost everything you need. Do something for a stranger. Not every stranger, and not in an attempt to be good or in a search for a cheap form of virtue. Do it just because.

Think. Take the complex fabric of your contradicting, tangled, bungled thoughts and grab a single thread of yarn and tease it out. Turn it over in your fingers and then ask yourself, like I do, how anyone could even consider that life could possibly be bullshit.

How Do I Deal With an Envious Friend?

I have a few times been in a position where a friend feels envious of me.

My initial reaction used to be to assume I had done something wrong, maybe been flashy with something bestowed upon me. The solution was to make myself smaller.

This never helped.

I learned I did not have in my possession the cure for the envy another person felt. You are not responsible for another person's emotions. You cannot control or change another person. You can only work on yourself.

I don't make less of the things I do anymore. I share both the wonderful and the not so wonderful things that happen to me.

I want friends who want the best for me and who are as happy about what I do as I am about their success and good fortune.

If that is not the case, if envy is what they feel, that's for them to sort out, not me.

I have enough on my plate with all the things I myself could be getting better at.

How Do I Deal With Family Members Fighting?

Hello. I am you. Future you.

The Peacemaker. That was my role.

I think I anointed myself.

Being the peacemaker involved being conciliatory, an intermediary, a mediator, a negotiator.

It involved intervening and doing my best to restore harmony to complex family dynamics.

It meant losing sleep over people's feelings getting hurt.

It was a full time job.

I was often accused of meddling and being nosy (because, I was). My answer was that I didn't want this but that it was necessary.

And therein lies the trap, doesn't it? How can you stop doing something that exhausts you and that you begin to suspect is probably not helping if it is also what makes you feel indispensable?

One fall day I decided I no longer wanted this responsibility. I reasoned that relationships that did not involve me had nothing to do with me, and that they needed to figure things out without my intervention.

183

It's been years and with the clarity of hindsight I can assure you everything is better. It's not healthy to be in the middle of everything. It's not healthy for the people that I love, "help" and "protect", it's not healthy for the relationships that I am trying to do something for, and most of all, it's not healthy for me.

Not Interesting

I have a friend who made a deal with her husband (and later, with her friends): *If I am ever saying something that doesn't interest you, just lovingly tell me you are not interested.*

This is less about my friend being dismissed while saying something that really matters to her — such as, *"this is how I feel"* — and more about the conversations we burden others with that we know full well are just chatter.

For example: too much detail about something transactional that happened during my day, long narrations about the entanglements of people you have never met, a convoluted explanation about something inconsequential that happened at the office.

"I am sorry, sweetheart, but that's not interesting" saves us both from what in the course of a marriage (or a lifelong friendship) amounts to months of pretending to follow a conversation, of acting engrossed when I am in fact bored, from having to nod and feign I am following, periodically muttering *"uh huh."*

"I am not interested" means I become aware of what interests me versus what interests us and can increasingly focus on conversations that are meaningful for both of us.

What Do I Say to Someone Who Feels Hopeless?

When I am happy I feel like I can spill my happiness everywhere, be messy with it, let it splatter, slosh, drown everything, everyone. Happiness is desirable, like sunshine.

When I'm sad I feel shut down. I feel like I have to make myself smaller, contain this sadness, hold it in, stifle it. It can't stain or contaminate anything. As if this was contagious.

My sadness wants to do what my happiness does. It wants to spill out of me, splatter everything, *don't you see, I'm so sad, I am hurting, this sadness is so big — help me — I don't know where to put it, how do I coop it all up, hold it back?*

I don't have the strength.

Dushka no, don't be sad, there is nothing to be sad about, look up, cheer up, buck up, pull yourself together.

And there I am carrying this burden that's so heavy and so much bigger than me and somehow I have to hold it up, hold it in.

This is why I think the best words to say to someone who is sad is *come here, sit here, set it down here, you are welcome here, you have space here to feel whatever, to be sad, be sad all you want* and maybe this way I wouldn't have to hold it in, I wouldn't be so scared about it touching anything, I could let it pour out of me freely, just drain out, leave me empty to make room, room to be happy again one day.

Why Do Friends Disappoint Me?

When I was in my teens I broke up with a guy I loved and none of my friends came over to see how I was doing. None.

Why was I so alone?

Later I was very busy with my first job and my friends constantly called me when what I wanted was time to myself.

Why didn't my friends understand me?

Just because someone cares for me doesn't mean they can read my mind.

And just because someone is my friend does not imply their life should revolve around providing me with what I need.

That's my job.

Expecting less from others and communicating clearly about the expectations that remain has lightened my relationships and saved me from the most isolating kind of suffering: the one that only exists in the stories I tell myself.

Can White Lies Hurt?

I don't like eggplant.

Imagine that one day a friend makes me an eggplant dish.

I pretend it's delicious in the name of being polite; in order to not hurt his feelings.

So now whenever I go to his house he makes this dish for me.

Over time this lie, like every lie, compounds.

I am not just lying. I am pretending.

How can I now explain that I actually don't like eggplant?

If white lies are a way to handle my relationships then eggplant is not the only thing I lie about.

Lying becomes an easy out.

It becomes increasingly hard for my friends to know what I like, what interests me — the real me.

It makes me wonder why I am so often misunderstood.

A "tell the truth" policy does not have to be rude, brutal or hurtful.

As you reveal the truth buried underneath a thousand misguided attempts to protect others you set your life back on a track that is true to who you are.

No Ill Will

Hatred, resentment, and ill will are poison. This is not a figure of speech. These feelings demand from your body a fight or flight reaction, releasing stress hormones that affect your immune system and raise your blood pressure.

They tether your thoughts and your energy to negative things and steal the light and splendor that is in everything.

It's not not worth it, this hatred. Forgiving is how you get rid of it.

Forgiveness means wishing the person you are forgiving no ill will.

It does not mean the person occupies the same place in your life; nor does it imply that you carry on as if the transgression never happened.

You can, for example, forgive someone and resolve never to see them again. You don't distance yourself out of anger or spite but out of respect for yourself; out of a healthy need to set new boundaries.

Forgiving someone is not a gift to the person who hurt you but rather a gift to yourself. It will set you free.

How to Recognize What Another Is Feeling

The next time you experience sensations like fear, isolation, sadness, abandonment, being misunderstood, remember. Remember this.

Remember everything: how it makes you react and how differently you interpret the things others say.

These feelings distort the whole world, don't they? They change everything.

Remember.

How do you look? Is your head down? Do you lower your eyes? Do you feel like not talking to people? Are you angry, abrupt, blunt? Is your wrath misguided?

Remember. Observe yourself.

This is how you learn to recognize these emotions and these reactions in others.

The more you are able to see yourself — at your best and at your worst — in others, the more you realize compassion is the appropriate response.

How Can I Make True Friends?

Appreciate your friend for who she is. Don't try to improve her, fix her, change her, interfere with her, rescue or save her, not even "for her own good".

A friendship is not a project.

Support your friend's interests with all your heart. Sometimes her interests will take your friend away from you. Support her anyway.

Be happy for her success. Not envious, not sorry she is doing better than you, not outwardly happy and secretly resentful. Sometimes her success will take her away from you. Be happy anyway.

Don't harbor grudges. This means speaking up, being direct, and giving your friendship the energy, time and attention any relationship requires.

Be there when it matters. I don't believe there is a correlation between how often you see someone and how close they are to you, but being there when it's important is friendship equity.

Listen. Listen without judgment and without the assumption that you are supposed to fix the problem. Just listen.

Follow through on what you say you are going to do.

Understand that a person's way of loving you is how they love. They will not love you your way. They will love you theirs.

Be true. To get anything at all you have to start by being what you are looking for.

How Do You Pick Your Battles?

I used to fight every battle, even the ones that weren't mine to fight. It's not that I had boundless energy. It's that not fighting made me feel like I wasn't standing up for myself, like I wasn't doing my feelings justice, or like I wasn't being loyal enough to a friend.

Like I had to make things right for everybody.

Standing down felt like a form of self-betrayal, like I was abandoning myself, so I raged, raged even against impassive, disinterested or immutable things.

As time went by I began to drop the battles I realized I could not win. I wasn't giving up but rather (slowly) recognizing my limitations and preserving my resources to expend them where they could make a difference.

I began walking away from the battles that felt like I had lost even when I won.

If you win but it feels like you've lost something of bigger value, does that count as a win?

I relinquished the battles that took too much energy, like look I won but now I am too exhausted for it to ever feel that way again.

Now, very, very few battles strike me as worth the fight. Who am I to be the judge of how things should be, of who is wrong and who is right?

Persuading anyone to see things my way has lost its luster. It's no longer interesting, when with that same effort and grit I could be learning something new, or creating something.

Being the Best

I am so very, very bad at bowling.

Every time we go, hopeful, persistent friends volunteer to teach me and either stand to my side so I mimic their movements or stand behind me to physically guide me into the proper technique.

Then I try to bowl, and *wow, Dushka. You really just can't — wow. Look at your score.*

In the bowling alley we go to there is a restaurant with delicious food, and after we play we sit around a big table and share what we ordered.

We laugh and talk and catch up, and someone comes around to pat me on the back and tell me that maybe some day my ball won't go straight into the gutter.

Some people in the bowling alley are really good. They are shy, or precise, or fussy — they ask everyone to be quiet — or perform, like entertainers.

They swing their arm back with flair, and swooooosh, the ball skids clean and straight and with a characteristic hollow clatter knocks down all the pins.

It's spectacular — the sight and sounds and lights and the smell of crispy French fries and worn shoes.

If I was better than everyone, I guess for a moment that would be cool, but taste the crunchy pickled radishes, and look at how handsome my friend looks with that sweater (I like men in sweaters), or watch how everyone at the next table high-fives each other.

Being the best? Nobody cares. That's not the point. It never was.

Why Is My Friend Stealing From Me?

I had a friend who kept taking things from me. The day I solved this problem forever was the day I stopped wondering what to do about her and began to wonder what to do about me.

Instead of asking "how can I get her to stop?" or "why is she doing this?" or "how should I handle her?" or "why does this betrayal hurt so very much?" I turned everything towards me.

Why, Dushka? Why is it OK to call someone who would do this a "friend"? Why do I have in my vicinity someone who would repeatedly hurt me?

Why am I betraying myself?

I decide who to allow in my life and in exchange for such a valuable lesson I let that friend keep everything.

Noble

I have many close friends and loved ones and frequently communicate with them through WhatsApp.

Mostly we text about logistical things (*see you Sunday at 7:00 at the soup place*) but often we have more complex conversations that stretch languidly over several days.

I like to wipe things clean so every week or so I go into the app and delete everything.

Sometimes before I do I re-read exchanges, in particular those that inspired me, intrigued me or said something that brought me pleasure: good news, a celebration, a compliment, a verbal snuggle, an "I love you."

Re-reading exchanges is always revealing.

I realize that there is more than one way to construe something. That I interpreted that in a way different than was intended. That the way I remembered what was said was not what took place.

We are unable to grasp things objectively. Everything goes through a messy filter of assumptions, insecurities and whatever we are carrying on that day.

Every one of our interactions is predisposed, prejudiced, ambiguous, inexact.

This is one of the many reasons I love language. We don't really understand one another, but it's so noble to try.

.

Is It Bad to Give Unsolicited Advice? Why?

Because I don't like being told what to do.

Because it feels like a form of power.

Because it feels like a form of control.

Because it feels like a form of dominance.

Because it feels like we are not equal.

Because it feels like you are establishing an authority over my own thinking.

Because I like to think for myself.

Because the expert on my life is me.

Because I want to be free to make my own mistakes.

Because it sounds like a veiled form of criticism.

Because it assumes you somehow know better than me on me.

Because I want your approval and your advice feels like the opposite.

Because it implies you don't trust that I can take care of myself.

Relic

I recently found myself in combat, fighting with someone over something I thought I deserved.

I think I felt I needed to stand up for myself.

I put everything, everything on the line.

Mid-argument, feeling stressed, exhausted, sad, disappointed — it hit me that I did not truly want what I was fighting for.

What I was experiencing was a misguided battle for something that used to be important to me but no longer was.

A relic.

It was time to let it go.

I dropped the fight right in the middle of feeling all tangled up in it. I lay my weapons down. I said I was sorry and explained where I was coming from.

The stress diminished. The sadness. The disappointment. Gone.

I feel free.

I am going to stop fighting over anything I don't actually want, and I wish the same for you.

Why Do We Remain Friends With People Who Hurt Us?

Do you know what? If I eliminated from my life all the people who make me feel bad, I would not only be alone — I wouldn't even have myself.

We (and by "we", mostly I mean "me") are clumsy, careless, thoughtless, say things we don't mean, say things we do mean uttered at the wrong time, say hurtful things when we are trying to be loving or helpful or god knows what.

I don't know. I don't know why I said that.

We are a mess. An inept, bumbling mess.

The thing to look at closely is intent.

Is the person who just hurt me wanting to hurt me? Is this person deriving pleasure from watching me wince? Do they put me down to feel better about themselves? Do they clip my wings the moment they show signs of sprouting?

Then I run.

But if what I have before me is someone who is occasionally graceless but with their heart firmly in the right place, I keep those people around.

Because I can be (and am) just as lumbering, and the people I love are generous enough to let the times I've hurt them slide.

203

Why Does No One Believe I Don't Want Kids?

The real answer to this question is really important and really difficult, no matter what your age.

If you hear me and make space for it, it might serve you well forever.

Here is the answer.

Ready?

It doesn't matter. It doesn't matter if anyone doubts you.

The trick is in wanting what you want, in not wanting what you don't want, and being so secure in your choice that you pay no mind to what others think or say or do, even if what they are doing is doubting you.

To be so sure of how you feel that even changing your mind does not concern you. To know that if you change your mind, and everyone you know says *"I told you so"*, that what you have decided to do is more important than the horror of proving everyone right.

The trick is in being perfectly comfortable with being doubted, with being misunderstood and with disappointing others.

In realizing that if you don't want kids or do want kids or go back and forth with this decision, you don't ever owe anyone an explanation.

Anecdotally, I knew early on I would not want kids. I have not changed my mind.

Paradoxes

The better you love yourself and the more comfortable you are with being alone the healthier your relationships are likely to be.

The more something irritates you in someone else the higher the chances you are seeing a projection of yourself.

Watch what you complain about closely. Watch closely what others complain about. Gossip reveals so very much about the person doing the gossiping. See for yourself.

The more you try to control another to forever keep them by you, to make certain they don't ever glance at anyone else, the quicker you will suffocate them and push them away.

The harder you try to be liked, be approved of, be popular, the further away these things will get.

You will have less of whatever you chase.

Anything you push will push you back.

You think you own your stuff. Your stuff owns you.

The less time you have to sit in silence the more you need to.

On that note, the less you feel like going to the gym the more you need to.

If you wait until you "feel motivated" the less it's likely to come. It's action that engenders motivation.

The more you try to manage your time, be productive, create color-coded grids to be more efficient, the faster time will tick tick tick away.

Everyone will have something to say about the choices that you make but nobody actually cares.

So, go ahead. Be you.

Offering

I love doing things for people who matter to me. If there is something I can do for someone in my life, I do: an introduction, a recommendation, assistance, a reference, a good turn.

Doing things for people I care about makes me feel lucky and buoyant but it also makes me feel capable. I can do this. I can do this for you.

A few days ago, someone did something for me. I didn't ask for it — it would not have occurred to me. It was a thoughtful, caring act and it had a very real impact on my life.

I am not usually on the receiving end of gestures such as this. It made me feel many unexpected things. Taken care of, which I have not felt in a long time since I insist on taking care of myself. Grateful — so grateful I felt a physical sense of expansion in my chest. Also, thrown. I felt off balance. Indebted.

I don't know how to repay you for this.

I discovered that doing something for someone is magnanimous, but allowing someone to do something for you is its own kind of generosity. It takes an open heart to know how to accept someone else's offering.

How to Say "I'm Sorry"

I'm bungled and flawed and clumsy and inadvertently hurt the people that I love so saying "I'm sorry" like I mean it is a necessary skill.

Nothing feels emptier than *"I'm sorry for whatever it was you think I did"* or *"I'm sorry you feel that way".*

That's like a gift box that holds nothing.

A heartfelt apology needs to assume responsibility and be delivered as soon as possible after the infraction.

As much as I would want to, this is not the time to dilly dally.

I try to be very specific about what I did wrong. I am so sorry I *— ate all the leftovers — snapped at you when you were an innocent bystander — got angry at you when really I was angry at me — I'm sorry I am in such a bad mood — I am sorry I was so impatient — I'm so sorry I wasn't paying attention.*

I then add a why to what I did. This helps the other person (sort of) understand me, which is useful for long-term relationships. It gives the other a sense of if and when this might happen again. *I came home late and I was so hungry — I was in a bad mood about something else — I wasn't clear on what was really bothering me — there are so many fascinating things happening simultaneously that I am easily distracted — I was afraid.*

Then I extend a peace offering. *I will make you dinner — get you flowers — listen next time without interrupting and without losing my focus — warn you if I'm grouchy about other things — tell you I'm scared instead of lashing out.*

Then I say *"I hope you can forgive me but you don't have to."* Because, they might choose not to and that's something I can neither force nor change.

How Do I Ask "Are You Okay?" to Someone Who Isn't?

If you ask someone *"are you ok?"* and you already know the answer, then your question is not at all what you want to say.

So pause and think about this — what do you want to say?

For me it might be — *can I take you to lunch?*

Or, *can I drop by your house with tea?*

Or even what I most frequently want to say when someone important to me is not doing well:

I love you. I just want you to know I love you.

Open Mind

I am categorical.

For me, it's yes or no. Black or white. In or out. Come or go. It is because of this that making decisions is easy for me.

To take it a step further, the wrong decision is, to me, better than no decision.

I considered this a symptom of strength and clarity of thought but time has taught me that being categorical is a form of inflexibility. It closes me off to so many possibilities. I miss out on things that demand I be more fluid, more elastic.

I have a friend who feels the consequences of something — even something drastic, such as betrayal or duplicity — and is able to experience pain without shutting off. He can swing back, like a trapeze artist. He can remember that this person who seemingly let him down is also the person who once did wonderful things for him.

This trait makes him resilient — resistant to the whims of others. It makes his relationships strong, increases his tolerance, helps him manage disappointment, forces him to carefully regard all sides and ultimately makes him suffer less.

It's a form of emotional generosity.

For me, and for many people in a culture of snap judgments, this is misunderstood, undervalued, foreign and difficult to hold, but look at it.

I have a tendency to instantly make up my mind. He has a tendency to keep an open mind.

What a superpower.

People who don't make up their minds can frequently confuse and frustrate people who just want to make up their minds. But the world needs more open minds. Not more categorical ones.

Cacophony

Tell me this:

If someone at work tells me that I need to go, that I am no longer needed, why am I so quick to assume this means I am not valuable?

Why can't I separate the painful life experience from my worth?

Why can't I say *"the fact you don't need me does not mean I am not necessary?"*

If someone says to me *"I don't love you"* or *"I don't love you anymore"*, why am I so quick to assume I am not worth loving?

Why can't I say *"the fact that you don't love me does not mean I am not just right for myself, just right for someone else?"*

If someone else puts me down, why can't I take it in and select what will build me up and discard what will tear me down?

The work, the big work, is to learn to listen to others while honoring my own worth.

The big lesson here is turn away from the cacophony of voices outside of me and learn to honor myself.

What Does It Mean to Take Things Personally?

I'm driving through traffic. Someone cuts me off. I am furious, feel attacked. I chase this other car down. I quickly catch up to the offender and see through the window not a vicious monster but someone dancing to music, distracted, oblivious.

Maybe he was driving irresponsibly but he was most definitely not trying to cause me injury.

I arrive at my office. I walk in and say hello to the person sitting at the reception desk. She turns her head away and does not reply.

I spend the morning wondering why she might be angry at me.

Maybe she doesn't like me.

I find out later she was wearing headphones and didn't hear me.

I call a friend and leave yet another voicemail. I wonder why he hasn't called me back. Clearly our relationship is not as important to him as it is to me. This fills me with sadness.

Suddenly I remember: he was going on a camping trip and has no cell phone access.

Taking things personally means interpreting that the actions of another are in relation to us when most of the time things that hurt us, insult us or worry us have nothing to do with us.

Not taking things personally means we make room for the possibility that not everything is about us.

This does not mean that things that aren't personal don't affect us, because they do. It means that we take the blow differently because our emotions are not all wrapped up in what happened.

This is important because by setting our ego aside we fight less, get angry less, feel offended less, suffer less.

Unimaginative

Judging others — how they act, what they say, what they wear — is a universal habit designed to feed our ego.

We make others small to feel big.

Look. Look how much better I am. Look how much better I do.

Judging is an unimaginative way to make ourselves feel like we belong. *Those people,* we say. *They are not like us.*

It underlines what makes us separate, instead of reminding us we are the same.

The act of judging comes from insecurity and is a symptom of unhappiness. If you are truly happy you don't need to cut others down to size or put down the choices others have made.

Speaking ill of others, even as a joke, as a way to pass time, shows people how you will one day come to speak of them and makes them wonder if you can be trusted.

The habit of judging is worth breaking for all these reasons but also because it continuously trains your brain to be critical. It narrows your vision.

You make it increasingly difficult for yourself to see the good in others, and consequently, the good in you.

Elixir

Do you know what the magical elixir is for me? Feeling heard.

I don't need action or help. I don't need to be rescued or saved. I don't need you to fix or change the circumstances. Just hear me.

If you ever wish there was something you could do for someone, here it is: listen.

How Can I Console a Grieving Person?

When someone is in pain, chances are they need to talk.

They need to talk and talk, because every time they talk they process, because every time they talk they untangle, because every time they talk they forgive themselves a tiny bit more for the role they believe they played in this horrible thing that has happened to them.

You don't need to do anything. You don't need to fix or help or adjust or clarify. You don't need to console.

What you need is to clear your calendar. What you need is to push everything else aside. What you need is to listen, just listen, and either intently, soundlessly think or even say out loud — there is no limit.

There is no limit to the amount of time I am willing to sit here and listen to you.

Rejection

Let me share with you what I've learned about rejection and about abandonment.

First, rejection is omnipresent. It's like air, all around me, something I can't get away from.

No, Dushka. Your contributions aren't good enough. We don't want the article you submitted. This won't work. I don't love you anymore.

The more I put myself out there and the more I recognized rejection as inescapable, the less of a big deal it was.

It became almost transactional.

You don't want this, that came from my very core? You sure? That's cool. Next!

The second thing I learned is that there is no relationship between rejection and my value. Which is to say that just because someone doesn't want me doesn't mean I'm not worth wanting.

You can reject my writing and, look at it. It's still good. You can reject my friendship and I'm still worth being friends with. You can leave me, and I'm still worth loving.

I'm massively flawed and a work in progress but also I'm certain of my inherent value, regardless of how you feel.

The third thing I learned was that we constantly make promises we cannot deliver. I have assured people I won't ever leave them. I've invoked the word "forever".

Every time, I forget that feelings are fleeting, and that any vow is likely to make a liar out of me.

When people say they will never abandon me and then they do, they're not failing me. I'm not a victim of their cruelty. They meant it when they said it. They just can't keep it — because it's unkeepable.

What I need to do instead of demand that people not hurt me is recognize others as fallible and ever changing, like me.

So, yes. I have been rejected and abandoned, and I am still here.

This is how I overcome these things, and how you can too.

Not Important

Many, many things make me feel I'm not important. It's easy for me to feel like I'm not someone else's priority (and, why should I be?) like I have been overlooked, like I am not valued, like I was not invited to the party.

Because this happens to me so consistently I decided some time ago I can't blame it on somebody else.

If someone makes me feel like I am not important I cut them some slack and work on myself.

I am tired of my expectations and the pain they cause me.

In every single thing that has the ability to hurt me I have to start by working on what I can both change and control, and that is one thing only (and only barely): me.

Now my assumption is that I matter a lot to you and that also you have other things going on that, alas, don't all revolve around me.

These Never Help

Calm down.

Stop it.

Stop crying.

This was you.

It was your fault.

You are so ___.

You don't know how to ___.

You never.

You always.

You are wrong.

What the fuck is your problem?

I do everything around here.

You're not there for me.

You don't make me happy.

I don't trust you.

Best Friends

The best friend you can ever find is one you never feel you need to lie to.

Weight

When I have a falling out with someone, I measure two things:

The weight of whatever caused the falling out.

The weight of the friendship.

If the friendship matters to me I push aside the falling out and look to talk to my friend as quickly as possible.

If the weight of the falling out is heavier than the friendship I turn my attention to the people I love and want to keep in my life.

Constant Validation

If I need constant validation, this insatiable yearning betrays a pattern of people pleasing and looking for approval that becomes my guiding principle.

This means that how others will react to my choices takes precedence over me listening to my own needs.

It means I will quickly adapt, shifting who I am to who I think others want to see.

It means I am hyper-intent on reading the behavior of others which implies I experience difficulty making decisions and take everything personally.

It means that what is familiar to me is a partner or a friend who is unreliable and who I have to chase. My relationships all have something in common: they are a roller coaster of emotions.

It means I feel stuck and like I don't have control over my life. This is because I truly don't. I have given away control in exchange for approval and love.

This is an extremely painful, absolutely exhausting way to live. Instead of grounded, secure, I feel tired, shifty, unlovable. I feel responsible for things I have no power over. I feel doomed.

To get unstuck, the only answer is to begin a practice that will change the way I live my life. There are no shortcuts. Believe me: if I had an easy answer, I would give it to you.

This practice has to do with noticing: look, I'm doing it again. I am doing this for approval, instead of doing it because I really want to, or doing it for me.

I don't berate myself. I am doing this because this is what I know, but I will, one action at a time, one day at a time, rewire myself, right down to my soul. This is not who I am. This is what I've learned, and I'm going to un-learn it.

Un-learning this will change everything.

This practice has to do with abandoning the notion that I have to help or fix others, or make others happy. It has to do with freeing myself from the arduous, futile work of managing what others think or feel.

It has to do with beginning to create something for me. Space to be alone. A morning ritual where I get up and take deep breaths and write. Sacred time to listen to myself.

It has to do with learning to create boundaries. Creating a boundary is really hard because it runs counter to what was once my guiding principle. It means putting myself first over getting another person to love me. (Throughout this process I will lose people. I will also learn that the right people will stay.)

It has to do with observing every habit, every action, and committing to taking care of myself. To giving myself what I need. *You need to be validated, Dushka? You need to feel you are not alone? You need someone you can count on? I am right here.*

I am not implying we do not need others. I am not describing a practice of selfishness or isolation. Make no mistake: to me, connection is the meaning of life.

What I am saying is that I need something steady to stand on to give the best of myself to others: not someone desperate, grasping, needy, but someone certain, solid, strong.

227

Everything Is OK

My brother is getting a divorce. He and his wonderful wife have two precious kids and are trying to navigate the situation as best they can. This is what my mom and I are talking about when she asks *"how do you think my divorce from your father affected you?"*

I told her that the divorce itself was not what had impacted me but the way certain things had been handled. She asked me for examples.

The first example I gave her was how my parents, in an attempt to protect me, would assure me that what I was experiencing was not taking place. *"No, no. Everything is OK. We were not really fighting."* Or, *"The yelling you heard last night must have been the neighbors."* I explained that when you deny a child's reality the lesson is I cannot trust my own perception.

I added that I knew this had not been her intention, that she was dealing with a lot and that she at every step had done the best she could.

I told her too that joint custody — constantly switching from one home to another — had been hard for me. I never spent more than 6 days under the same roof until I was in my late twenties.

We talked about many other things too: how difficult it is when each household has different rules and you have to keep track of who you need to be. How I always felt I was betraying a parent if I enjoyed the company of the other. How I felt it was my job to make sure everyone was getting along. How hard it is to deal with other relationships as parents start dating.

My father's girlfriends had a tendency to tell me about the problems they were having with my father. I felt honored and involved and responsible and loved being confided in and treated like an adult. I was nine.

I came to terms with all these things a long time ago and am aware of (many of) the patterns I have in my own life. I don't hold any grudges towards my parents, who truly were the best parents I could have asked for.

Even then, talking about all this, feeling heard, the confirmation of many things I remember and that had never been validated, and witnessing the fact that my mother was curious and receptive, rather than hurt or affected by what I was saying, was an enormous gift.

Why Are People Judgmental of Introverts?

People will judge you no matter what you do or who you are.

If you had the super ability to swap your personality at will, you would be judged for who you are and then be judged again for whoever you switched into.

You would end up standing in the middle of a room spending all of your time and your super ability desperately flashing from one character to the next, a powerful shapeshifter unable to ever find the shape to satisfy everyone.

People are not judging you because you are an introvert. People are judging you because people judge.

So, you might as well be who you are.

Big Thing

Do you know what's a small thing that's really a big thing?

Energy.

Pay special attention to how you feel in someone's company.

Awake, happy, inspired, thoughtful?

Exhausted, drained, perplexed, maybe even like you can't trust yourself?

Hang out with people who make you feel like *yah*!

And, doesn't it make sense to distance yourself from who depletes you?

Should I Stop Pleasing People?

I have a confession to make.

I like people-pleasing.

I like doing things with and for other people, in particular when it feels like a joyful, natural co-creation, in particular when giving something of me feels like the best use of what I have to give.

It's the best.

I just have to be careful that I don't swing from "I feel open and generous towards you" to "I feel resentful because I have come to see it's not how you feel towards me."

I don't want to feel like what I do is being taken for granted or like I'm being taken advantage of.

Every relationship I have is built on certain principles. I get to know someone and natural dynamics are established. If I have always people-pleased and I decide I want to stop it with the people-pleasing, if I want to stand by me instead of feeling resentful, I am in essence altering — betraying — the tacit rules of our original arrangement.

I used to say yes to everything and now I am putting me first. It stands to reason that this will shift every single one of my relationships.

The people who react to this first are, obviously, the people I've been bending myself for the most: this is where my change is most noticeable. They don't like it, because they have grown comfortable with getting everything from me. *No, Dushka. What has gotten into you? Let's go back to the way things were.*

If these people value me they will come to realize that a new balance has been in order for some time and that my new rules are only fair.

If they instead value how convenient I made everything, how comfortable they are benefiting from me overextending myself, the relationship might not recover.

At first, this hurts like a fire in my heart.

But then, then, as the pain begins to recede, look at all the space I've made. Look at the room I have, the energy I can put into relationships that are better for me.

I am recovering, and now I feel free.

See, I made it so easy for you to use me, and now my life is better without you in it.

So, yes. Discovering who you are, shifting into being fully you, is a tough, painful road. But let me tell you. It's the best thing you will ever do, both for yourself and for the people in your life who really matter.

Do You Like Nice or Truthful Friends?

This question is hiding a belief that will hurt me.

It suggests that being nice and being truthful are a dichotomy and that I have to select one or the other.

That if I choose veracity people around me will not be nice.

That if I choose nice then I will have to live in a world where things are not what they seem.

I'd like to suggest that maybe the truth is just the opposite.

That lying is not nice.

That you can be sincere and not hurt me.

That I can (and in fact do) choose friends who are both honest and really kind.

Has a Friend Betrayed
Your Confidence?

One day I told a friend a secret and she went and spilled it to
somebody else.

At first I was furious.

Then I realized it was a misguided attempt to support me.

"Betrayal" is a very strong word. It hurts. It's an assault, a
violation of trust. It makes me feel both shattered and indignant.

Like *how could you.*

Like *you broke something and it cannot ever be put
back together.*

Before I call upon this painful word, I review intent.

What was my friend trying to do, when she was revealing what I
had told her in confidence?

Why? Why did she do that?

After taking a closer look at what she had done, I was still angry.
I still told her that I did not like her transgression.

But, it was less of a betrayal and more of an indiscretion.

This is how I suffered less, and how our relationship survived.

He Says He's My Friend but Acts Like He's More

If someone tells me they only see me as a friend it's best if I believe them.

They are using clear words and have no motivation to lie.

If I'm interested in them, my brain wildly encourages me to see things that aren't there.

This is the power of wishful thinking: it makes me disregard someone's very clear words and replace that clarity with what my brain tries to convince me must be "signs."

This is how I break my own heart.

Friends are playful with each other. Friends by definition enjoy and search for each other's company. I try to stand right next to my friends. Sometimes I throw my arms around them and tell them I love them.

None of these things is an implication of anything more — in particular after someone has made it clear they just see me as a friend.

If you think I'm wrong, then ask.

"You said you saw me as a friend but I feel you are saying one thing with your words and another with your actions."

Then you can hear the answer for yourself.

It's better to hear a clear answer than to allow my brain to take me on the savage roller coaster ride of trying to decrypt how someone feels about me.

No Free Passes

One of the main ingredients of a happy life is the practice of boundaries.

Exercising them means exercising them. It doesn't matter how people react to them, and it doesn't matter who the people are.

Many times we allow our boundaries to be trampled on because the person who tramples on them is family. Because, *"family is everything."* Because, *"blood is thicker than water."*

We are stuck in believing family automatically deserves a free pass.

An absence of boundaries is unhealthy, and particularly unhealthy within the dynamics of family.

This looks different inside of each family, but some examples of poor family boundaries are: abuse that is hard to identify because it's what you've always known, family members being extremely involved in matters that for you are private, the sense that you are responsible for everyone getting along, a parent insisting you be who they wanted to be, instead of who you are.

Keeping your family away is something only you can decide. Nobody needs to understand it, support it, or approve of it but you.

The decision might make you feel awful, because if you've never had clear boundaries they make you feel like you are being disloyal or failing someone important to you.

But, boundaries are key to your mental health. It will help teach you to listen to your own voice, to decide how you want your life to be, to show yourself that there is no reason why your upbringing has to be your destiny.

It helps to remember boundaries are never fixed. They shift, and pushing someone out of your life for the sake of your health does not have to be forever.

How Can I Strengthen a Friendship?

Friendship was part of our original composition.

It was designed when we were designed, and as such is indivisible from our central nervous system, our muscular capacity and our mitochondria.

This means it existed before office buildings and before our restricted notion of modern chronology.

Friendship happens when we hang out, when we stroll, when we have nothing to do. It also happens when we schedule and plan and limit get-togethers to an hour, but these things are less natural to something that is more primal.

My favorite time with a friend is when we clear an afternoon and have nothing to do. We stroll, aimless, and talk without search or goal or outcome. I return home with a full heart.

Looking back, these are the times that have most contributed to cementing my relationships.

If I'm Polite With Someone I Don't Like Does It Make Me Fake?

Of course not.

In Mexico, where I am from, we have a saying: *lo cortés no quita lo valiente.* (Courtesy does not make you cowardly.)

"Polite" suggests civility, basic good manners.

Not liking someone does not imply you should be rude or inconsiderate.

Or, acting impolite just because you don't like someone makes you ill-mannered, ungracious.

Self-Care Quick Tips

Rest is not a luxury.

Boundaries are not selfish.

It is not necessary to explain or apologize when setting a boundary.

Making demands on what someone else can give you is not respectful.

The need to be right is ego driven.

Winning an argument is shortsighted.

People-pleasing is not the answer.

Saying no is necessary.

Resentment feels like you are angry at someone else but really it's a sign you have compromised yourself.

Taking on someone else's emotions is not empathy.

What is familiar is not always what is healthy.

You can always change your mind.

"I need to be alone" does not mean *"I don't want to be with you."*

How people behave is related to themselves (not to you).

Criticism is just an opinion.

You cannot control what another person is going to do.

Blame = powerlessness.

Feeling triggered is the path to healing.

You are not responsible for another person's emotions.

The magic of deep breaths is always available to you.

Grief belongs to you.

The most valuable thing you can give is your attention.

What people want more than anything is to feel seen.

How Can an Introvert Feel Comfortable With Many People?

This introvert (me) feels (sort of) comfortable hanging out with multiple people:

When they are all people I love. For example, my own party is less exhausting than another person's party. (That being said, I decide I want my own party maybe once every five years.)

When nothing is expected of me. I am not there to "network" or "work the room" or "meet people" or hand out business cards. I refuse such assignments. Why show myself to everyone precisely when I am at my worst? There are other ways to meet new people that play to my strengths.

When I am in the company of an extrovert. The talented, effervescent extrovert happily, naturally does all the work and I stand there and contribute rather than carry the conversation. Keep a few extroverts handy for such occasions. I can't recommend them enough.

When I can prepare. For example, I message people before the event and say I want to catch up with them. Then I can focus my attention on meaningfully talking with, say, four specific individuals, and let everyone else fade into the noisy background. Even when I can't prepare, determining to have a few good conversations rather than many quick ones helps a lot.

When I can take breaks. I step outside. I hide in the bathroom. I (physically) lean into my extrovert and sigh.

When I give in to the fact that I am going to be uncomfortable. Just because something makes me uncomfortable doesn't mean I always have to run from it. Making peace with a situation is less painful than fixating on avoiding it.

When I can plot a smooth getaway. If I am at the mercy of, for example, the time when one of my beloved extroverts wants to leave, then I feel I can't get out and snap into a code red.

Everyone Takes From Me

Whenever I feel like "everyone" does something to me, I know I cannot hold the world responsible. There is something I am doing that is causing a behavior that keeps replicating in others.

This doesn't mean I am to blame, that it's my fault, but rather that I have the power to do something differently so that this stops happening to me.

Let me tell you what I do that results in feeling like people keep taking from me: I continue to believe I am responsible for others. For how they feel, how they are doing, what they do.

I can help.

I think this is because I have a deep, underlying belief that if I am "helpful", if I am useful, if I can fix someone, then I will be needed and loved.

If I can play a role in making things better for others, then I matter.

If all I do is try to help and get involved and, well, meddle, this inevitably results in me feeling resentful, used, abused, taken for granted.

I cannot control the emotions of others. I cannot help others, but I can help myself. The day I learn to establish healthy boundaries is the day people will stop taking and will start giving back.

That day is up to me.

No Trace of a Grudge

Have you ever gotten food poisoning?

You like shrimp and eat one and get horribly sick. You spend a few days feeling like you might die. Slowly, you recover.

The next time you see shrimp you can't. You just can't. Stay away from me.

This imperative — stay away — does not go through my heart. I don't hate shrimp. I don't feel resentful towards shrimp. I don't harbor ill-will towards it.

It's not intellectual either. I am not rationalizing or thinking. I'm not even using words. Just recoiling.

There are people in my life (fortunately, very few) that have hurt me that I have completely forgiven. I feel no trace of a grudge. But my system has identified them as poison, and as such I will keep them away from me.

Who Do You Love the Most?

Ach, no.

It makes me sad to even think about doing this.

It requires playing favorites, or quantifying love, or putting relationships that matter to me through a process of elimination.

I mean, why?

Relationships are not on a gradient. Love is not linear. Feelings are not constant. What I feel for each person I love is unique and different and often feels total.

Presenting myself with this question forces me to pretend I am comparing apples to apples, when in fact every single one of my people is gloriously different and gives me different things. No one else is my mother or this sister or my father. No one else is my brother or this niece or that niece or this friend or that friend or even that person I just met. No one can give me what this person gives me.

There is no one, no one under the sun quite like you.

Every relationship is my most important relationship and my heart holds congregations, an army, a throng. You don't need to ever fall in line. I won't ever number you. I won't pick someone else over you.

I love you all the same, and different, and a ton.

Do You Fear Having Your Heart Broken?

No. I am going to die no matter what I do. If something is going to kill me it might as well be love.

What Is the Best Mindset to Go Into a Relationship?

No one can rescue me, save me, complete me, change me or make me happy but me.

We are not responsible for each other's emotions.

Drama is not interesting. There is no jealousy, wrath, abuse, blame, grand gestures or emotional addiction.

We set clear boundaries, and respect the boundaries of the other.

We both work at identifying our expectations and our assumptions.

The more clearly we communicate, the better our partnership.

We are open about the things that hurt us.

We are invested (rather than afraid of) the growth and evolution of the other.

We are OK with being uncomfortable.

We are OK with things being awkward.

We understand that triggers are something to work through, not something to run from.

We understand it's normal to feel attraction towards others.

We do not attempt to control, manipulate, own, dominate the other.

We keep our word: to ourselves and to reach other.

We both benefit from independence.

We both want and need time alone.

What Should I Think of Me if Someone Manipulated Me?

If a beloved friend was manipulated I would do my best to show her that I love her. I would support her. I would treat her with both compassion and care.

I would tell her to carefully review the ways in which she was responsible, to reduce the chances of this happening again. I would remind her that there is a marked distinction between taking responsibility (which would empower her) and assuming blame (which would diminish her).

I would advise her to guard her heart from ever hardening, from becoming suspicious and mistrusting. Closing her heart would not protect her. It would isolate her, which is the last thing she'd need.

Do you know instead what I'd probably tell myself? That it was my fault. That I was blind. That I should have had the sense to see this coming.

Then I'd remind myself that these things are not true.

More importantly, if I realize that I am treating myself or talking to myself in a way I would never do to anybody else, that's when I know I'm way off base and must recalibrate.

Remind me. What would I do for a beloved friend? This is how I'd work on treating myself.

Why Doesn't My Boyfriend Text Me Back?

I walk into a yoga class and feel so stiff. I spent Thanksgiving weekend with my family in LA and have not done yoga for several days. I worry this class is going to be difficult, that I am not going to enjoy it.

I feel stiff. That's a fact. The rest is just a story.

My co-worker is acting aloof. *Is it me? Did I do something to offend him? Is he mad at me?*

It's true my co-worker is aloof. The rest is just a story.

I text someone and he doesn't text back. I spin out. *Why isn't he texting? Does he not care? Does he not want me? Is he not interested? Is he with someone else? Why is this happening to me?*

It's true he is not texting me. The rest is just a story.

Be aware of the things that are fact and the things that you add. Whatever it is that you are adding is just a story.

I know that sometimes the suffering is in the thing, but mostly, it's in the stories.

Indecisive

I have a friend I admire for her strength, resolve, her intelligence and her determination.

These same traits can make her rigid, intractable and difficult.

Intelligent people often experience their intelligence working against them.

She and her boyfriend are going through a hard time and in her mind there are two options: to stay, or to go.

"But, what if you tell yourself that for now you don't have to decide?" I say. *"What if the answer is to do nothing, until things become clearer?"*

"I can't do that," she replies. *"I am a solver. I need to close this now."*

"OK," I say. *"What if you decide, and embrace that your decision is not permanent? For example, you can decide to stay, and understand you can break up later, or decide to break up, and understand you can get back together."*

"No," she says. *"I'm not like that. I stick with what I decide."*

How can I argue with who she is? And, how can she? She's trapped. She's trapped by the way she defines herself.

But, isn't who you are supposed to serve you? If something about yourself is not serving you, you cannot regard it as immutable. You have to be more fluid with who you are, if that's how you might suffer less.

What she needs is to be indecisive. My friend, a problem solver, a lover of certainty and definition, needs to waver and be tentative and vacillate. She needs to learn to gently hold uncertainty and lack of closure. In doing so she can keep both her relationship and the possibility of no relationship. In this pre-decision discomfort, she can have everything.

Do Low Expectations Mean We Settle?

I come from a time and a place where women were expected to be good housewives. The expectation was that I'd have children, run a tight ship, cook well and have dinner served promptly.

I would deeply disappoint anyone who expected these things from me.

An expectation is the assumption another person is going to act a certain way. Expectations have nothing to do with the person we expect things from, and everything to do with ourselves.

Expectations are at the root of every disappointment.

Expectations can be very disrespectful towards another person, who, alas, is not what I want him to be or who I believe him to be, but who he is.

I want to be aware of my expectations, so that when someone doesn't do what I assumed he would, I can tell if he is disappointing me or if I am disappointing myself.

I have very high standards for my relationships. I want clarity in communication. I want both of us to know how to distinguish what is our own problem with what is the other's.

I don't want to strive to meet someone else's impossible expectations of me — I want instead to be loved for who I am. This is what I in turn will do for another.

Grounded expectations. High standards.

Is Casual Dating Healthy?

I have a friend who enjoys casual dating. She meets people and can keep things light, can manage to neither demand nor expect more than what's right in front of her. Casual dating for her is fun, entertaining, and as such, healthy.

Despite efforts to the contrary, there is nothing casual about me. People fascinate me, and being fascinated means intense curiosity. If I feel transfixed, I want more, not less, and before the other person can say "no strings attached" I'm already weaving something.

I'm a total involvement kind of person. I don't do anything casually, and if I try I end up getting disappointed, hurt, and whatever the opposite of fun is. (Torture? Agony? Misery? Distress? Anguish?)

For me, casual dating is not healthy.

Liquid

Love is not constant. It's not steady. It's more like an ocean, rippled, turbulent, wavy, inconsistent, unstable.

It's a liquid.

Neither I nor my relationships can be at the mercy of my emotions. I simply don't have the stamina to always be riding the wild roller coaster of my inner landscape.

When someone is important to me, I look past what I feel right now and get a good look at the person. Is this done, or do I want this individual (friend or lover) in my life for the long haul?

I hold this fluctuating quality of emotions and let the ups and downs move through me so that I can attempt to be the things my feelings are not: consistent, regular, reliable, unbroken.

Meeting in Person With Someone You Met Online

Life is risk. If I don't take any, my existence becomes lackluster, limited and circumscribed.

But I have to calibrate, measure this risk. How can I expose myself to the good, reduce the chances of something bad happening to me?

If I had a conversation with someone on social media and felt like meeting them in person, I would.

Here are the things I would keep in mind:

I would be aware of signs of manipulation. Is he trying to emotionally entangle me, saying things disproportionate to the amount of time I have known him?

I feel like I've known you forever. I can sense this becoming a real thing. Wow. I have never met anyone like you. Any of this is a red flag. It's not that I'm not special. It's that he doesn't know me. I would block them.

Is he trying to goad me? *How brave are you? How open minded are you? How adventurous are you?* Block.

Any request for financial support. *I have a sick child, I am stranded, I have no one but you.* Block.

If our exchange seems healthy and natural, I would meet him in a public place with other people present, not somewhere secluded.

I would say no to any form of isolation. I would not get in a car — even if after a good date he offers me a ride back to my place.

Is this overly cautious? Maybe. When going back and forth on how to calibrate risk, I want to err on the side of caution.

Here is another flag: if someone has good intent they WANT me to feel safe. So they would say something like *"is there a public space you would be comfortable meeting me in?"*

If I say *"I am not into getting a hotel"* and he replies with *"Why? Don't you trust me?"* Block.

You are supposed to make me feel safe and of course I don't trust you, on account of the fact that as good as this might feel I don't know you.

Healthy relationships both respect and encourage basic boundaries. The most basic of them all is my comfort and safety.

I can't control the world. The best I can do is be smart with the choices that I make.

Builder/Destroyer

To me the great builder of any kind of relationship is an expression of interest.

What do you do when you are interested? You tune in. You notice. You listen. You pay attention. You are curious.

It's very beautiful to see the world through someone else's eyes, to participate in something you wouldn't normally because it really wasn't my thing but now that I know it's your thing I'm suddenly quite keen. Yeah. Let's go.

It's also very beautiful to feel seen, the sense that someone else is attempting to get to know you, traverse the range of your inner landscape, the dazzle and the hazards.

The great destroyer is contempt. Nothing shrivels any relationship like having someone regard you with disdain.

Do I Have to Tell My Boyfriend Everything?

My life, my relationships, my stories, my secrets all belong to me.

I get to decide if I want to share them, and if so how and with whom.

As I decide, I establish my boundaries. *"I love you, but I don't feel comfortable talking about that." "I appreciate your curiosity, but I prefer to keep that firmly in my past."*

My boundaries are my own, because they relate to my life and my limits. This means no one can demand that I move them. I'm not obligated to tell anyone anything.

How much I decide to share will influence the level of intimacy of my relationships. If I safeguard a lot, I will keep everyone at an arm's length.

Secrets are a form of isolation.

I am not implying this is good or bad. That would depend on you and what you want out of your interactions with others.

I was full of secrets. There were many, many things I did not want to share.

These secrets created an ivy-covered labyrinth in my brain: a complex series of compartments and ins and outs and walls and closed doors and shuttered windows.

Through the years I have slowly shared my secrets. I have found that the more I share, the less power they hold over me. The more walls come down. The more doors are left unlocked, or ajar. The more windows swing open.

The more I share, the lighter I become.

The Most Difficult Part

To me, the most difficult part of any relationship is the ability to tell the difference between the other person's problem and my problem.

My ability to feel valued is a really good example of this.

Does this issue of feeling valued present itself across many of my relationships?

Do I think I am valuable?

Do I value myself?

The answers to these questions might indicate where the problem lies — in his treatment of me, or in my regard for myself?

The reason this distinction is important is because if I place the issue on him when the problem is me, I will cycle through one good relationship after another, seeing the same thing present itself over and over again.

I have found it's always better to begin with me.

Fantasy

I can say I love everything, everything about a person before I get to know them well.

This is because I love who I imagine them to be, not who they actually are.

As I get to know them, who they truly are begins to replace my fantasy. And then, ugh. I guess I sort of love them, but they are irritating, annoying, selfish, thoughtless, whatever.

Because, why are they who they are, instead of what I thought?

Why do they love me how they love, instead of how I imagined they would?

Why don't they do what I expected?

And, even worse, why are they so disappointed with my inability to be who they thought I was?

How am I supposed to know who it is that you need me to be and how could I be someone I am not, even if I wanted to?

Be careful when you say you love everything about a person. Make sure that who you love is the other, and not your fabulous overactive imagination.

Because, that's not love.

That's projection, and it's what we do.

If He Never Texts Me, Does He Love Me?

I have a tendency to measure another person's love using my love as a calibrating instrument, the measuring tape, the reference point.

If I love people, I text them frequently so if they don't text me they must not love me.

This is a fallacy. People love in all sorts of different ways. Someone can madly love me, love me well, and never, ever text me.

What I perceive as a lack of effort becomes exactly that: my perception, not objective lack of effort.

This is a tragedy because it makes another person's love invisible to me. You say you love me, and I just can't see it.

What a waste.

At this point, I have two choices:

The first is to make peace with the fact that people do not love me the way I love or the way I want them to love me. They love me the way they know how.

The second is to find someone who is compatible with me, who loves me in exactly the way I expect. I go and find someone who texts me a lot and shows me love in a way I interpret as such.

The first option opens me up to a rich, polychromatic, abundant world of many different kinds of love. The price is that I have to constantly remind myself that people don't love me the way I want them to.

I surrender. Just love me. Love me any way you can.

The second option comes with the ease and flow of a common language. The trick is that just because someone is doing what I have grown used to and come to expect, it's no guarantee that they feel what I think they do.

In other words, he can text me all day and not love me at all.

When I'm Thinking About Someone, Are They Thinking About Me?

When I can't stop thinking about someone, it feels like my thoughts are spilling out of my head and splattering all over everything. Everything.

Of course this means he feels the same way. How couldn't he?

When I am grieving, what I expect is for the world to stop. Stop everything. Even the clocks. In words of W. H. Auden —

The stars are not wanted now: put out every one

Pack up the moon and dismantle the sun

Pour away the ocean and sweep up the wood.

How dare the sun still be shining when my insides are all darkness?

When I am angry I stomp around certain I can slam every door with my thoughts. Knock over the vase on the coffee table. Blow the windows out with my fury.

This is what my very convincing feelings do — they make me assume nothing else exists, and that others for certain feel what I feel.

Do you know what makes me inconsiderate, disrespectful, self-centered? Believing my feelings. Assuming you feel what I feel

271

because I feel it means I leave no room, make no consideration, for what you might feel.

If I feel passionate about you and I kiss you without asking, this is me assuming we are one, expecting you want what I want.

I am taking for granted an absence of boundaries: I am believing you have none.

So yes, when I feel, it feels like you feel. But, I don't know what you feel. You are not me. You are a whole different person, and my feelings — even my powerful, overwhelming feelings, even when they are true and certain — my feelings stop with me.

Northern Lights

The thing that scares me about a relationship is our tendency to confine ourselves in the name of making room for it.

There are many things left for me to discover, many things I am interested in, pursuits that might become a part of who I am, different women inside of me who are jostling for the chance to unfurl and express themselves.

Instead of nurturing all this, which is in effect my life force, I will turn my back on it for "us".

So that you are not threatened, so that you feel safe, I will extinguish things that make me feel alive: I will deny my (very real) feelings of attraction towards others, make less of my (frequent) crushes, will not flirt (when flirting is life affirming), I will turn a blind eye to all the beauty around me.

I will not make time to go see the Northern Lights.

I will diminish me — when I want the result of who we are together to be something that expands both you and me.

What I want is an arrangement designed to defy this — where we both grow, learn — stretch instead of wither.

I don't want to do everything together. I want you to have your life and for me to have mine with the added joy of being interested in the life of the other. I will not be interested in many things you are interested in, but I will unfailingly be interested in you.

I don't buy into the notion that commitment has to mean detention, confinement, obligation or a burden.

I am committed to who you are and to who you can be rather than committed to the things that bind us, or to the sacrifices we convince ourselves we must make for each other.

I don't want us to dedicate our lives to managing each other's insecurities.

I want you to inspire me to create, to express, to explore, to discover, and I crave knowing I inspire you in the same way.

If this sounds good to you, that's awesome. If it doesn't, that's awesome too.

I clearly see this is not the kind of thing I can convince another person to want. It can only work if it happens to be the place you have arrived at too.

Can Casual Dating Lead to a Relationship?

I don't want you (or anyone) to get hurt so I'm going to tell you something. I'm going to tell you, but alas, telling you will be an exercise in futility.

You're going to go ahead and get hurt anyway.

Here we go.

Of course casual dating can lead to a relationship. It's entirely possible, and even common.

But if someone says "I don't want anything serious, let's keep it casual" and you enter this agreement thinking "he says he wants nothing serious but this can totally lead to a relationship" it means you are not listening.

It doesn't mean you are ignoring a "flag" — it means someone is spelling it out for you, and you are overriding it.

So, here we go. Here is the very useful, totally futile thing I want to say and I will say it even if you will instantly toss it aside: If someone says "I don't want anything serious", please believe them.

How Do I Learn to Kiss?

You learn to get things right by doing them wrong and doing them wrong and suddenly midway through doing them wrong you — stop. Stop. Just stop.

This is how I get them wrong. I need to do something differently.

You don't learn to live by reading about life, by wondering about it or by asking yourself how on earth it is you can finally stop procrastinating on all the things you want and don't want to do. You don't learn to live by contemplating the many ways that you cannot. You learn to live by living.

You don't learn to trust by regarding everyone with suspicion and wondering how it is that you can manage to always remain safe, safe behind all of your excuses. You learn to trust by trusting.

Kissing is delicious. It is one of my favorite things. Spending a whole day kissing would be an excellent use of my time. And you can practice on a pillow, I guess. But mostly, you learn to kiss by kissing.

Just Look at You

People develop crushes on other people for all sorts of reasons.

Someone says or does something particularly insightful or interesting.

Someone exhibits a quirk that catches your eye.

A peculiarity snags on your heart.

Oh my god. I just want to look at you.

Sure, you can crush on someone because he is good looking but I can assure you looks are not the only reason humans crush on others.

On a related note, both beauty and ugliness are subjective.

When I love someone their looks matter less than zero because they look absolutely beautiful to me.

How to Impress an Experienced Man

Did you know that sex with each and every person is completely different?

What the person likes, prefers, what turns the person on, what the person might be interested in or open to.

Everything. Everything is different.

Which is to say that even if this man has allegedly tried everything and is very experienced, what is new to him is you.

You don't need to do anything in particular to impress him. Explore him. Enjoy him.

As far and wide as either of you have been, you are new to each other, and you is all you need.

I Love Her but Am Afraid to Tell Her

This is a universal, ubiquitous, pervasive choice. It will follow you everywhere you go, present itself in every decision you ever have to make.

It will be right there waiting for you day after day, with lovers and friends and family. It will mark the path of your career.

This right here is what draws the line that is your life.

What will it be today — fear or love?

The more you choose fear the more your life will shrink. The more regrets you will have. The more your vocabulary will be *"I should have"*, *"I could have"*, *"What if I had?"*.

Fear begets fear. The more you tell yourself *"I can't"*, *"I am unable"*, the more that will become your truth.

You will be blind to the fact *"I can't"* is something you have chosen rather than something that is real.

The more you choose love the wider your life will become. The less you will wonder what could have been. The more you will have around you the people and the life you dream of.

The more *"I can probably do that"* will be your truth.

What you do next is up to you.

Is Staying Single Bad?

The last time I was in a relationship was about a year and a half ago. We broke up because, although we loved each other and have remained close friends, we were massively, irreconcilably incompatible. Living together meant years of constant, relentless friction that exhausted us both.

Over the last year of our seven year relationship I fantasized about having my own space. I wanted more than anything to live alone without having to push against anyone to express my preferences, the way I wanted to live, and, ultimately, who I was.

After we broke up I did move into my own place, which was painful and lonely and also felt like heaven. As part of my "getting my life back on track" effort, I went on a couple of dates. They felt unnatural. The regular rhythm of my life is to be in a relationship, and this time I was shocked to realize I wasn't ready. I decided that what I needed was a long, deliberate hiatus from dating.

During this time I have put a lot of thought into what it means to love yourself and make room for who you are. (I wrote a book about it: "Love Yourself and Other Insurgent Acts That Recast Everything.")

I have felt scared and lonely and gone through painful things without coming home to anyone but me. I have become (relatively) more aware of many of my patterns and beliefs. I have spent time with my amazing ex, now my dear friend. We are proud of the enormous effort we both made, and marvel at how much better our friendship is now that we don't have to put up with the unintentional tyranny of living with each other.

I've also noticed how being single is something other people resist or attempt to fix, as if it was a problem. *"You are single! Wow, I'm going to introduce you to someone!"* or *"how can someone so wonderful not be married?"* or *"don't worry. He's out there somewhere. You will find him."*

The fact is that I'm single by choice, that it's my preference, and that the idea of the presence of a man in my life for now feels like more than I can handle. I don't know how long is too long. I don't want to begin a relationship driven by anxiety (*My god! I am getting older and will never find anyone!*) rather than by love.

It's OK to be single. It's OK to take your own sweet time. It's OK to make space to sort yourself out and get to know the person you have become underneath that relationship (or series of relationships). It's OK to navigate through the angst and the fear to learn you don't need anyone but you.

Being single is not a limbo between relationships. It's not a state of temporary suspension. It's here. It's now. It's everything I need.

Dating Fundamentals

If you like someone and would like to get to know them better, ask them out.

During the date, be who you are. If you say you like something that you don't like or act differently than who you are, at best the other person cannot get to know you and at worst might like the person you are pretending to be.

You pretending to be someone you aren't is not sustainable.

Be tactful but clear about how you feel. *"I really like you and would like to see you again."* Don't say *"I will call you"* to 'be nice'. Keeping someone waiting or expecting something that is not going to happen is not nice.

You will hear a lot of advice about playing hard to get, not calling the person back right away, or hiding your feelings.

Keep in mind dating is the beginning, and the beginning sets the tone for the relationship. I would shoot for one that is honest and simple, not one fraught with pretending and games where I never really know where I stand.

Do you think the person you are with is not being clear? Don't read between the lines. Instead, ask. *"I'd like to see you again. Do you feel this way too?"*

Remember the meaning of consent. Don't make assumptions. Do you want to touch her, kiss her? Ask.

Your feelings are your own. Just because you have a crush doesn't mean she has a crush.

Remember you can't control another person and you can't own another person. I know this sounds obvious now. It won't always be obvious so I thought I'd just remind you.

Stay safe. Always let someone know where you are and who you are with.

During the date, listen to yourself. Do you feel strange, threatened, unsafe? Never push past that. Never ignore that. Never try to reason with your instincts. (Don't do this: *Wow. I feel creeped out. This makes no sense! He/she seems perfectly nice!*)

Dating is supposed to be fun. It's less about finding "the one" (there is no such thing) and more about meeting new people with an open mind. Focus on that.

Distracting

I find good looks insanely distracting. I see a long row of red flags and *I mean, look at his soft brown eyes. And look at how he carries himself. Look at how he looks at me. Yes, I want to go out with you! Let's just push these pesky red flags out of the way, here. Stack them over there in the corner. Come on in.*

I've done this so consistently that now just the fact that someone is good looking puts me on high alert.

Conversely, remember that just because he is good looking doesn't mean he's not right for you.

Relationship Boundaries

Get clear on what you want and what you don't.

Get comfortable disappointing others. Getting approval or another to like you is the enemy of a clear boundary.

Understand that having boundaries is healthy, not selfish.

Say yes or no devoid of ambivalence.

Listen to others so you respect their boundaries too. Respect begets respect (or should).

Remember: if it's your body or your property, you decide. You are the boss. *"No, I don't want sex tonight."*

If it's another person's body or property, that is not a boundary, that is controlling. *"If you don't have sex with me tonight ... ".*

Boundaries are not static. They change so you have to be attuned to what you want and what the people around you are comfortable with.

How to Tickle

Each and every body is completely different. Different bodies like different things.

This means one guy could say *"no, no, don't touch me there"* while another to that very same action could say *"oh yes, more of that please".*

To me, this is something worth paying attention to: learning what someone you love (or are attracted to) considers pleasurable.

For many people, "tickle" is synonymous with "torture" (which is cool if it's what you both are shooting for). For others, "tickle" makes them laugh and sounds like fun.

Alas, I can't tell you the best way to tickle someone. What you can do is tickle him in different ways and closely observe how he reacts.

Ask questions: *Does this feel good? Bad? Do you want more, less? I can do this again if you ask me to.*

Go discover.

Exploring is quite possibly the most fun you'll ever have.

Why Won't He Marry Me?

Because he doesn't think marriage is important.

Because he doesn't want to get married.

Because he wants to get married, but not to you. You can love someone very much and not consider them marriage material.

Because he feels like marriage will lead to complacency, evenings in front of the TV and an absence of sex.

Because he feels marriage will lead to him making compromises he doesn't want to make.

Because he does not feel comfortable with the legal and financial implications of marriage.

Because he values his own space and his sense of independence, autonomy and freedom.

Because he — like most people — is massively turned off by threats and when he hears he will lose you if he doesn't marry you he feels more rather than less reluctant.

Why Do People Go Back to Toxic Relationships?

I used to believe jealousy was related to love.

If he is jealous, then clearly it means he loves me.

This is a toxic belief. It betrays the fact I am most comfortable with men who are jealous, as this is what love means to me.

This pretty much guarantees I am going to end up with someone who considers me a possession rather than a person, who wants to own me, control me, who has a tendency to get irrationally angry if I am in the company of another man.

I intellectually determine that this is a pattern and I try a relationship with a man who trusts me, and who most of all trusts himself. This new man believes he is worth loving and knows that me finding another man attractive, flirting with another man or even finding another man interesting does not threaten him.

I know in my head this is right but in my heart I feel —

Alas. I feel unloved. Alone. Empty. Isolated. This well adjusted, incredibly healthy relationship is so foreign to me.

It does not stick.

And that is why people go back to toxic relationships.

Anxious Attachment

If my form of attachment is anxious, I want to be with the subject of my affection as much as possible, think about my relationship pretty much all the time, and think that anything my partner does is related to me.

For example, if my partner is with his friends I think *"he prefers his friends over me!"* rather than thinking *"it's normal to sometimes want to be with your friends".*

If he doesn't text me, I think *"he doesn't truly love me, oh no!"* rather than think *"life is about many, many things, not just staring at your phone".*

If I am anxious, I need to remind myself that I am not the center of the world.

I am not the center of the world. Things happen for reasons other than someone's feelings for me.

Reminding myself of this is a gift because it results in me suffering less.

It's good for my relationships too. Letting my anxiety drive my relationship results in turning every relationship I am in into something heavy, suffocating, toxic.

Better to let air in.

What Does a Soul Mate Feel Like?

It feels like the sudden glorious unfurling of every possible red flag.

It feels like I watched too many romantic comedies, listened to too many pop songs, and swallowed it all hook, line and sinker.

Never swallow things whole.

It feels like I believe everything will be perfect, like I will finally be happy because someone else can make it so.

No relationship can withstand this amount of expectation.

It feels like I need to hold on to my white horses, take it slow and determine to believe only what is real.

It feels like I need to remember that if I fabricate a person in my imagination then when that person isn't what I dreamed it was only me deluding myself.

We break our own hearts.

It's not that I don't believe that fantasies can come true. It's that real life is better.

What Do You Look for in Your First Date?

Ease.

I want the experience to feel smooth, effortless. I want to be able to talk, laugh, order food without friction, without tension and without awkwardness.

If things are strained and difficult, the rigidity constricts beautiful things. If instead the dynamic is fluid, it lets other things in: chemistry, friendship, good conversation, a second date.

Holding Hands

I love holding hands.

I love the gentle (or tight) clasp, the warmth, the rhythm.

The fit. My god — the fit.

The skin. Warm and soft and rough and alive. We are alive.

Look at us, walking in the sun.

I love the sway, the sweep, the give, the lock, the possession, the belonging.

I love the touch.

I love that I fidget and you hold me tighter like *no, where do you think you're going*.

I love that I am talking to you but only half paying attention to myself. Because really all I feel is where your fingers are threaded into mine.

And yeah in my heart I hope to be a teenager forever.

Because, back then it was you and me. You and me.

Why Do People Lie in the Beginning of a Relationship?

Because I am afraid.

Because I'm not sure who I am will be enough.

Because I want to seem better.

Because I want to seem unique.

Because I want to appear more interesting.

Because I want to be your type.

Because I want you to think I think like you.

Because I want you to see I like what you like.

Because I want you to like me.

Because I'm not quite sure who I am.

Because I don't really know what I want.

Because I'm trying to adopt the shape of your expectations.

Because I want to be the person you were hoping to find.

Who Do You Love So Much You'd Take Them Back No Matter What?

This question hides within it a lethal blind spot.

Can you see it?

This question assumes that taking someone back "no matter what they did" is related to my amount of love to them.

Taking someone back after they have done something terrible is not an effect of massive love.

It's an effect of low self-esteem and poor boundaries.

I can't control what I feel towards another.

If they hurt me, I will leave, and my departure will have nothing to do with the depth or size or sincerity or earnestness of my love.

I'll leave because I love myself, because I deserve more than "no matter what". And, so do you, my friend. So do you.

He's Not Ready

If a guy told me he loved me but was not ready for a commitment, I'd give some serious thought to my own feelings.

How do I feel? What do I want?

If I love him and am not ready for a commitment, we are both in the same place and can give this time.

If I love him and want a commitment, we want different things and are not compatible.

It's not a crime to want different things. The fact he is not ready for a commitment does not make him the bad guy. It does not necessarily mean I should stay away from him.

Where he is at matters in relation to where I am at so I need to be honest with myself (and with him) about what I want.

(For example, if I pretend to be cool and casual when instead what I want is a commitment, I will suffer and be unhappy and it will be my own fault for saying one thing and meaning another.)

Finally, I would consider it a really good sign to be with a guy who is clear and forthcoming about his intentions.

Why Are Good People Unlucky in Love?

This is a trap disguised as a question.

It contains within it a hypothesis.

If I choose to believe it, my relationships are destined to be unhealthy.

It implies: I must be cruel to be lucky in relationships.

This is simply not true.

My guess — and it's just a guess — is that we confuse a "good heart" with someone who has not set clear boundaries.

An absence of boundaries is not "nice". It's not related to goodness or selflessness. It's related to not believing I am worth loving.

My fear: if I lay down my boundaries people might not like me.

As I learn to establish boundaries, people who knew me as a person who always said yes and who always tried to please others will react, since they are seeing someone different from who they are used to.

Oh my god you have changed so much.

They might stay or go, but my firm boundary setting will begin to attract the right kind of people. The kind of people who respect who I am and the rules I establish for interacting with me.

Good hearted people treat others with compassion, with love, with kindness. This begins by being compassionate, loving and kind to yourself.

This ability to begin with you is the definition of selflessness: it's only from this place that you can dedicate your efforts to serving others.

Is He Friendly or Does He Like Me?

This is precisely why language was invented.

So you don't have to wonder, so you don't have to attempt to read signs you don't fully understand, so you don't ever feel confused or like you have to guess what another person is thinking.

Thanks to language, you don't need extrasensory perception.

I would say something like *"I can't tell. Are you friendly, or do you like me?"*

If you're lucky, maybe it's both.

Moving On

If instead of resolving conflict you move on to a new relationship, the same conflict will reappear, over and over.

Given enough time, the conflict will come into full blown focus, will become the center of your attention, while the people that you love will fade, fade into the background, become indistinguishable, merely a backdrop for this growing thing you are not resolving.

A new relationship will at first lend you the illusion that you are deft, nimble, a talented escape artist. Let me tell you. You can't run from conflict. I know this because I've tried.

How Do I Commit Without Losing My Freedom?

This question is about boundaries.

Start by defining what "commit" means to you. Forget about what it means to others. How do you envision it? What about this word makes you feel devoted rather than bound, willing rather than obligated?

Then, define what "freedom" means to you. Forget what it means to others. What do you want? What makes you feel trapped, stuck, cornered, unfree?

Once you are clear on those things, communicate your boundaries. An example might be *"I am committed to you, but I don't want to live with you. I like my own space and as such prefer to live alone."*

Or, it might be *"I am very committed to you, but I want an open relationship where we can see other people."*

Or, *"I want to marry you, live with you, not see other people, have a family with you, but I feel trapped when another person constantly tells me what to do or tries to control me."*

Different people are comfortable and happy with different things, and to "commit to a relationship without losing your freedom", you have to define it, and find people who define it similarly.

What Is Emotional Abuse?

If someone tries to make you small, to isolate you, threaten you, control you, to make you feel shame, if someone affects your dignity and your sense of who you are, that is defined as emotional abuse.

If someone swears at you and says horrible things, intentionally misunderstands you, makes fun of you, attempts to make you feel intimidated, and blames you for the behavior, that is emotional abuse.

Emotional abusers tend to establish dominance and then say they are very sorry. This is a cycle that tends not only to repeat itself but to escalate.

Emotional abuse undermines your self-worth, like subterranean devastation. It does not get better. You cannot end it by "being on your best behavior" or by "acting impeccably" or by "not provoking". This is because the abuse is not in what you do — it's in the abuser.

She's Angry Because I Need Time Alone. Am I Wrong?

I need a lot of time alone.

Through the years, I have learned that *"I need time alone"* is what I say, but that is not what others hear.

What they hear is:

Wanting time alone means you don't want to be with me.

Wanting time alone means your feelings for me are not strong enough.

Wanting time alone means you don't love me.

Wanting time alone means I am not your priority.

What this takes is communication, patience, education.

I try something like this:

"Maybe you are angry or hurt because you feel me needing time alone means I am not interested enough in you. Actually, it is not related to you. I had a long day and don't feel like talking."

This kind of conversation helps people understand each other better.

It helps people suffer less.

Because, think about it. She is not experiencing you being tired — she is experiencing you not caring about her.

Ultimately, if she needs a lot of your presence and you need a lot of time alone you might not be compatible — but before getting all the way to a conclusion of incompatibility, there is space. Space to work with.

What I want to say more than anything is she is not wrong in wanting more time with you, and you are not wrong in wanting time alone.

The real questions are — can you be patient with each other? Can you meet in a place that works for you both?

Can this effort open her up to not taking things personally — a lesson that will improve every part of her life?

Can it open you up to being better about how you communicate — a lesson that will improve every part of your life?

At its best, this is what love does. It changes us in a way that makes our whole life better.

My Relationship Is Temporary. How Can This Hurt Less?

Every relationship is temporary.

Nothing is permanent — nothing.

Everything we have is a gift, beautiful and perfect, and it's full and complete right here, right now.

He has not left. He is here in your arms and you can nuzzle him while he kisses your neck.

Right now this does not hurt. It in fact feels wonderful.

Right now you have the very thing you will later fervently wish for: his presence.

Don't squander what you have, which is certain and true, for fear of what you might or might not experience later.

One day, when he's gone and you are still here, only now without him, you will look back and say to yourself *"I loved him. I wasted no time anxious about later. I squeezed the best out of every moment I had with him. I did that well."*

And that's how it will hurt less.

I'll Never Love Again. What Do I Do?

After every relationship I've ever had I am certain I am through with love. I will never love again, which makes me feel despair.

That is when I realize that the future has not yet taken place. As such, whatever I think about what it will or will not bring is just a story.

I exercise coming up with another story that directly contradicts this one that brings me despair.

For example, I have a heart filled with love. I have learned so much from this relationship that I can apply to the next one so that it's better. And, you know what? I was so in love, so now I know my heart knows how to do this thing that is so scary. I won't have to wait as long as I've had in the past because now I know better. I've done better.

Is this second story plausible? It is equally realistic?

I actually think *"I will never love again"* is a bit excessive. *"Now that I know better I will love better"* is pretty pragmatic. More than plausible. Entirely possible.

I now have two stories that are equally viable. One makes me suffer. The other makes me happy.

You get to decide which one you want to believe.

How Can I Stop Caring About My Careless Boyfriend?

Whenever I care about someone who is careless with me I remind myself my feelings do not make me powerless. My feelings do not decide what I do or who I surround myself with.

If I care about someone who is careless with me I don't wonder how I can stop caring. I do all the things I can do, even if I care.

I break up. I distance myself. I get busy giving myself all the things he couldn't give me.

I can't control my feelings so I keep caring about him but with each passing day I care a tiny bit less. I recover. I heal.

In doing this, I teach myself that I cannot wait around for my feelings to align with the kind of life I want to live: healthy, vibrant, with people who care about me as much as I care about them.

On the other end of this, looking back at the person I finally don't care about anymore, I wonder what on earth took me so long, and why I believed this would take care of itself.

Why Do We Stay With People We Don't Love Anymore?

Because we feel we are what we used to be.

Because we hope we can get it back.

Because we are convinced there is no one else out there for us.

Because maybe this is as good as it gets.

Because there are other things besides love, like commitment and vows and the promises we make.

Because feelings change and I might love him again.

Because "familiar" feels safe.

Because our lives are intertwined and it's easier to stay.

Because leaving has an impact on other people, not just on us.

Because better the devil that I know.

Because what if I leave and realize I've made a terrible mistake?

Touch Panics Me but My Girlfriend Insists. What Do I Do?

I am so sorry this is happening to you. It sounds incredibly distressing and painful.

You needing to be warned before being touched is your boundary. It's your body — so you have the inalienable right to determine the rules of if, how and when you are touched.

It doesn't matter what anyone thinks.

The people you let close to you need to respect your boundaries. You don't ever need to explain or justify yourself.

What you can't do is change another person. You can't have any expectation of how your girlfriend is going to behave.

All you can do is say something like *"you need to warn me before touching me. I am sorry to say this is my boundary, and therefore not negotiable. If you can't respect it, I cannot be with you."*

I know this might feel really scary but you (and everyone) deserves to have people around you that respect what you are clearly stating are your personal limits.

Give yourself that. Give yourself an important first step in your own health: the ability to articulate and hold your boundaries.

How Do You Feel Secure in a Relationship?

If I fear I am not good enough this will pollute the way I perceive things.

If I try something new, for example, and do it badly, a secure person might say *"I had no experience! I need to try again!"* without a trace of discouragement.

An insecure person might say *"I can't do this because I'm bad at everything and I don't know why I even try."*

To feel secure in a relationship, you have to feel secure in yourself.

What Makes an Emotionally Distant Person Attractive?

He told me he was not looking for a relationship and instead of hearing what he said I decided he would change his mind.

It will be different with me.

He will change for me.

I can fix this.

I can save him.

I like a challenge.

I was raised by someone emotionally distant and this is me, replaying my patterns.

Because I am too afraid to truly be in a relationship and finding emotionally distant people is the way to keep myself safe. In other words, the emotionally distant one is me.

Because I don't really believe I am worthy of being loved so this seems to be the best I can do.

Because the flashes that are good are amazing and feel like such a rush and before I know it they've become the fix.

Because being in and out and the yes and the no equal drama and drama is what I think love is. No drama/no passion, right? (Wrong.)

Because if I could just adjust this one thing, he would be perfect for me.

How Do I Get Over Losing Someone Who Didn't Respect My Boundaries?

The scariest thing about setting boundaries — and the reason why sometimes I am not assertive enough — is that they might cost me my relationships.

But, someone willing to cross my boundaries is saying *"I am willing to get what I need at the cost of what you need."*

They are saying *"Your discomfort or you overextending yourself is OK if I benefit from it."*

Maybe I needed better relationships.

And that's how I get over losing someone.

How Do You Fix Yourself in a Relationship?

Relationships are a very good place for me to quickly identify what it is that I need to work on.

We can make a pact to support each other's evolution.

I can commit to my own health and well being and feel supported by someone with similar commitments to himself.

With my significant other, I can work on boundaries: what they are, how it feels to enforce them.

I can practice communicating as clearly as possible.

I can practice being vulnerable, talk about how things make you feel.

I can become aware of the things I do to try to control another person and begin learning how to work on myself instead of blaming or manipulating.

We can both work together through triggers (in loving relationships it's common to have a knack for pushing each other's buttons).

Finally, I want to say I don't agree with the word "fix". There is nothing to fix. I am not broken. I am whole and capable of growth. This is also true for you.

This evolution puts us in a place where we are responsible, accountable, can work on ourselves and consequently suffer less.

Why Do People Stay in Emotionally Abusive Relationships?

Because he doesn't hit me, or only does so once in a while, so how can this be abuse?

Because after he is terrible he is wonderful and there is nothing quite like that.

Because it feels intense.

Because it feels like love.

Because it's what I know love to be.

Because I'm hooked.

Because I don't know anything else.

Because it feels like loyalty.

Because I am not worth anything more than what I have now.

Because I need him.

Because I don't know how to untangle myself from this.

Because this will change.

Because if I leave he will hurt me. In fact, he might kill me.

Why Wasn't Jennifer Aniston Enough for Brad Pitt?

I never answer celebrity questions mostly because I don't follow celebrity news.

I am answering this question specifically because it hides within a toxic belief that is worth clarifying.

People don't leave people because they are not enough.

People leave people for reasons related to themselves, not the worth of the other person.

As paradoxical as this sounds, if someone leaves me it has little to do with me.

Untangling self-worth from being dumped is a crucial first step towards mending a broken heart.

Why Is Breaking Up So Difficult?

Because I don't want to hurt you.

Because I don't want you to hurt me.

Because I had dreams for us.

Because I remember the good parts.

Because why can't I get it right?

Because why couldn't I make this work?

Because isn't love supposed to conquer all?

Because what's wrong with me?

Because what if I'm not right for anybody?

Because we said we wouldn't give up on us.

Because I don't want to feel I've wasted all this time.

Because I don't want to break the promises I made.

Because if I stopped loving you what does that make me?

Because what if I make a mistake?

Because I am terrified of being single.

Because I am scared I will never find anyone else.

Because what if I am unlovable?

Because what if this is something I can't recover from?

Uncommon Addiction

Let's say that I come from an emotional family.

Things had a tendency to be impassioned, sentimental, fervent. Voices were often raised. Tears were spilled. Accusations cast. Doors slammed. Reactions were instant. Declarations were irrational.

Later in life, a steady, solid relationship feels meh. Tepid. Lukewarm. Changeless.

This is boring.

I fail to recognize that what is afflicting my solid relationship is that it's (gasp!) *healthy.*

That feeling trusting and safe is good.

And that I have trouble identifying all of these exotic things because I've never known what they feel like.

I am addicted to drama.

Drama — instant declarations of undying love, gigantic gestures, deciding immediately that I've found my soul mate, impulsive behavior — is not romantic.

These things are red flags, and what I need to see is that what I have identified as "love" needs to be — well.

At the very least, adjusted.

What Is She Feeling When I Stare At Her?

We don't know.

We don't know her or what she is feeling. We don't know why she is looking down, what she is thinking when she is smiling to herself.

We don't know if she's lost in thought or thinking of a man she loves or of someone she can't have or if she can in fact hear your voice.

We don't know and can never know if she can feel you staring at her.

Gather yourself. Gather yourself and walk over to her and say *"I'm so curious about you. I'd love to get to know you better. Can we talk? Can I sit here with you and get to know you?"*

Begin. Begin a lucid, easy life of clarity, accuracy and definition.

Please. Stop guessing. Stop speculating. Stop doing things that lead to murkiness and gloom. Stop thickening simple things with layers of assumptions and the impossible expectation of needing to read someone's thoughts.

We were granted the gift of language, free of shadows. It's bright and certain. Use it. It will change your life.

How Do I Know if I'm Settling?

You don't like being alone, so any relationship is better than no relationship.

Your relationship doesn't feel right (you *feel* confined, uncomfortable, exasperated, trapped, uncertain) but your thoughts convince you that it is (*Dushka, it's really not so bad*).

Your thoughts lie to you, but your body cannot. This is why it's so important to tune into your body.

You think this is as good as it will ever get, which is you being guided by your insecurity rather than by reality.

Instead of a fulfilling sense of peace or a sense of feeling grounded you are waiting, searching, hoping for someone "better".

Your bar is really low. (Well, he's not abusive.)

Your relationship lacks a sense of ease, contentment.

Things aren't great, but I've already invested so much.

You feel no sense of certainty and are instead constantly asking yourself if this is really the person you want to be with.

You don't love him the way he is but just as soon as you can fix him he will be great.

When you think about the future, he's not in it.

When you think about the future he's in it and that feels terrifying.

How Can You Recover After a Long Term Relationship?

I'm not going to sugarcoat this for you. Long term relationships are hard to recover from.

It's for this reason that I would try to have a lot of love, patience and compassion for myself. *Dushka. You loved him, and so much of life is about love. Good for you. Be sad. Mourn. Grieve. Be heartbroken. All of these things are OK, and it's OK if they take time.*

I'd make a list of things that I set aside for him. What are they? Maybe I was interested in learning to dance, and he wasn't, so I never did. Or, maybe there were places I wanted to visit that I left for later since he wasn't that interested. Maybe I liked nature and he was a city person. There is a special sweetness in recovering the things that were yours — like they've always been there, loyal, waiting for you.

So many things are waiting for you.

I'd take the love and the time and everything I gave him and give it to myself. All of it. The happiness. The joy. The sharing. The compromises. I would not jump into another relationship until I gave myself time to figure out who it was that I set aside all those years.

You are in for the discovery of the best relationship of your life: the one with yourself. There she is, under layers of oversight and inattention. There she is, under years of neglect. You will find her and dust her off and polish her and bring her back to her full radiance and luster and you will see for yourself. She is wonderful, and a thousand percent worth loving.

How Can I Make My First Date Memorable?

We don't know. Nobody knows.

This because "a good date", a "memorable date" and "good company" are all subjective. Different people define them in different ways.

I can make a few general suggestions.

Be present. Pay attention. People like being seen, and noticed, and considered interesting. For example, you listening to her rather than you looking at your phone.

To note: people are more interested in being considered interesting than in finding others interesting. I find this a big insight.

Don't pretend to be someone you are not. If you say you love roller coasters and you really don't, you'll have a hard time pretending you like roller coasters in the long term. In general, as you pretend to be someone you are not for others, you in effect begin to surround yourself with the wrong people, and find yourself in the wrong life. Why surround yourself with people who seek inversions and wild rides if what you love is when the ground is steady and firmly under your feet?

If by being who you are the woman you are with concludes she does not want to see you again, you have successfully accomplished the goal of the first date, which is to determine if this is a person you'd want to spend more time with.

How Do You Get to Know Someone?

Every boyfriend I'd ever had called me every day.

I didn't think about this or even consider that it was possible for there to be an alternative.

Later, I dated a guy who for a few days didn't call me. I was perplexed. I was hurt. I concluded he didn't care about me.

Him not calling me was not intended to be hurtful and was unrelated to his feelings for me. Calling every day was just not something he did.

I realized we had never spoken about how frequently we would contact each other. I took for granted what he would do, not because of him but because of what I was used to, before he even came along.

This was not terribly fair.

The fundamental thing to do to get to know someone is to get your own picture of him out of the way, so you can see him for who he is, and not for what you assume or expect him to be.

This is really hard because most of the time our assumptions and expectations are invisible to us. We don't realize we have them, much less that they are blocking our view.

Any flash of self-awareness feels to me like a shock, painful, startling, electric. Which I guess is a way of saying that after all these years I don't even know myself.

Is Not Wanting Children Selfish?

Ugh, see?

This is precisely why I think the concept of "selfish" needs to be entirely reconsidered. *"You are selfish because you are doing what is right for you instead of what is right for me"* — well. I can't get behind that.

Having children is huge. Huge. If I had children it would completely change my life. It's not something I can give to another, no matter how selfless I am or how much I love them.

Not having children is huge — huge. If I really, really want them and don't have them this will leave me with a big void forever. It would not ever be something I'd want to take away from a person I love.

Couples who deal with this — one wanting children, the other not wanting children, have a huge issue to overcome.

What I can tell you is that wanting children is not wrong. And neither is not wanting them.

He Treats Me Like Rubbish and I Can't Leave Him

No matter what I write, you will break up with your boyfriend when you are good and ready, and that's OK.

What I want to say is that this is precisely how you learn to love yourself.

When you feel someone is treating you poorly and know you should not be the target of poor treatment.

When you feel you are walking on eggshells for someone and recognize you should not be living like that.

When you tell yourself *"I can't bring myself to do this"* and suddenly *"I just can't"* becomes *"I can't believe what I just did."*

You walk away and it hurts so much and instead of telling yourself *"my life is over"* you say *"I feel like crap right now but eventually I will heal, and this is how that healing begins."*

Then, slowly, you start to learn to set boundaries and stand up for yourself. You stand up for yourself and stop feeling like you have to betray yourself to keep people in your life.

Every single time you do that, you recover. You reclaim yourself.

You start walking away from the notion that you have to sacrifice yourself at the feet of the people that you love. You stop trying to control what another person does or feels. You stop needing another person's approval: what you need is to approve of yourself.

Everything, everything you need — to be treated well, to be loved for who you are, to be seen, to be appreciated, to be believed in — you have to start by giving to yourself.

I understand how deeply you feel you can't bring yourself to do what you know you need to. But you can, my friend. You most certainly can.

Does Love Shown in Movies Exist in Real Life?

Have you noticed how people travel in the movies?

Airports are clean, the line to check in is short, flights are never delayed, suitcases are tiny even though characters change clothes frequently, days are sunny, skies are blue, museums are nearly empty and allow for conversation and leisurely strolls.

Does travel exist in real life? Yes. Is it wonderful? Yes. But it's full of friction that you never get to see in a movie.

So, yes. Movie love exists in real life. Except in real life, it's not sanitized for your viewing pleasure.

Closure From Recent Heartbreak

I'm going to tell you how to get closure.

It works, but it's really hard.

First, I recognize I am agitated. I need to let out some of that energy. I need to do intense exercise. I lace up and go for a run. I go for a swim. I go do some weights. I go to a yoga class. (Please don't do this without checking with a doctor.)

Second, I learn how to regulate my breathing. Deep, deep slow inhales, slow, long exhales. Do it again. And again. This doesn't work immediately but I keep at it. Your own breath is going to save you. You have a life-saving mechanism within you at all times. Doesn't that stun you with its beauty?

I meditate. Find an app that teaches you how.

Then — and what I am about to tell you will sound preposterous and impossible, but stay with me — I attack all of my wrath and anger with a mega powerful anti-rage nuclear device: gratitude.

I make a list every day of all the things I am grateful for. Thank you for ripping my fucking heart out and stomping on it. Thank you for teaching me about pain. Thank you for teaching me about loss. Thank you for hurting me with your callousness. Thank you for making me wonder every day how I didn't see this coming.

Every day, 5, 10, 15, 20 things. I make them different every day. I slowly transform my fury into gratitude. It changes everything. Everything.

And, the last point. Compassion. Towards myself. *I love you, Dushka. I love you. I love you even when you become this person that would be easy for me to hate or feel ashamed of. I love you just the way you are, all your flight and excess, your ferocious, unreasonable heart and your ravenous desires. I love you. I love you and am terribly sorry for the role I played in putting you in this place of pain. Let's get out of this. Let's go.*

It's Scary for Everybody

Once, years ago, I told the guy I was dating *"it sounds like you want things to be over, so let's just make a clean break."*

He said *"OK"* not so much because he wanted a clean break but because he thought I did and wanted to respect my boundaries.

When I said it, we were fighting, but I wasn't angry. I was afraid. I craved reassurance. I was hoping he would say *"a clean break from you is not what I want"* and make me feel safe again.

The problem with pushing people away in an effort to be soothed is that my relief comes at a high cost: it steals all the safety away from the other person.

There is a price to every game we play.

What I had to do was precisely what terrified me: call him and apologize. I told him I loved him and that this love made me feel like my security was constantly on the line. I said I was sorry for pushing him away when what I wanted instead was to feel that he wanted to stay.

They say love conquers all but even two people being careless or clumsy can destroy everything.

The guy forgave me, but the incident taught me that I need to be very careful with what I do and say to the people that I love. The people who love us are just as scared as we are.

My Boyfriend Talks About His Ex. Should I Be Worried?

You should not be worried at all. Not one bit.

Let me tell you how it is that I can make such a declaration despite the fact I've never met any of you: because no amount of worry on your part will have any impact on whatever it is your boyfriend is feeling, or planning to do about it.

Here is what I would do in this same situation. I would trust myself. I would trust him. I would make room for the possibility he might still have feelings for her, and that having lingering feelings over someone does not necessarily impact how he feels about me.

I would make an effort to be secure and confident, and proceed as if I expected everyone to do the right thing.

The alternative is for me to worry sick, to be madly jealous, to be super insecure — which will make me suffer (possibly needlessly) and might even push him right back to her.

What happens if I am secure and confident and he leaves me for her? Well, being madly possessive and jealous would not have stopped that. And leaving me for her would make him a cheater, and through the whole thing I would know I handled myself with grace — not to mention, I set myself up to suffer as little as possible.

336

What Should I Do if My Relationship Is Falling Apart?

You have three choices —

One — To hold on, continue on the path that you are on and be a witness to the collapse of your relationship.

Two — To identify the patterns and the central problems that make you fight, and do everything differently. This requires that you reconsider your own priorities, that you find the issues that you bring into the relationship and do the work, both individually and together.

When you make this decision, you don't do it for the other person. You don't do it for the relationship. You do it for yourself. You realize that who you are is not working, and that you've had enough.

In words of D.H. Lawrence —

Are you willing to be sponged out, erased, canceled, made nothing? If not, you will never really change.

And in words of Julio Cortazar —

Nothing is lost if you have the courage to proclaim that everything is lost and that you must start over.

Your third choice is to call it a day, and leave.

Why Do I Still Miss Him if I Was So Unhappy?

Whenever I meet someone new my brain spins a story about them. It's a powerful cocktail of fantasy, wishful thinking, and pop culture programming. Shake. Pour.

When the relationship ends it feels like I miss the person — but really what I miss is the person I fabricated. I miss a figment of my imagination. I grieve over the left over splinters of a delusion — not really over the broken relationship that ended up being nothing.

The fact that I miss a ghost does not make the missing any less painful.

My brain is incredibly powerful. The only antidote to her ability to deceive me is to learn to distinguish the thoughts she thinks from who I am.

This learning is not a single dose lesson. It's a practice. I return to it every day.

How Can I Stay Away if She Hurt Me but I Love Her?

What works wonders for me and diminishes my suffering is to be less categorical.

I add the words *"for now".*

Rather than *"I want her out of my life"* I say *"for now I don't want her in my life".*

This means I am giving myself what I need right now but am also open to the possibility that how I feel might change (or, might not).

This is also much easier for others to process. *"I love you but for now I need some distance. Thank you for understanding."*

How Is a Heartbreak After a Non-Relationship?

Heartbreak is heartbreak.

Labeling a relationship is a social construct. It's intellectual. It's done with words. It comes from my head. It's a decision.

Regardless of what I determine to call it, my feelings go right ahead and place that relationship or non-relationship in their rightful emotional place.

When the whatever you want to call it ends or fails or disintegrates, it doesn't matter what my brain decided it was.

Maybe aside from the usual pain I add a side dish of anger for being stupid enough to believe I could protect myself by calling my relationship nothing.

What Hurt Will You Never Get Over?

I don't buy into this.

I am resilient. I bounce back. Some things will take longer than others but my plan is to heal from anything that ever hurt me.

I think you can too.

Anxious

Hello! My name is Dushka Zapata and I suffer from anxiety.

I am anxious pretty much all the time.

What this means is that I don't just feel anxious when I have something specific to feel anxious about, such as a job interview.

I feel general anxiety over I don't know what. I worry. I fret. My thoughts become catastrophic. I go to the worst case scenario. I obsess over small things. I have trouble sleeping.

I lie awake certain that I will lose everything I love.

In an effort to feel better, I have learned something incredibly powerful: to disbelieve my own thoughts. To regard any feeling as fleeting. To soothe and calm myself.

I write any thoughts that help me surmount this anxiety and share what I write hoping my readers find that what has soothed me can maybe soothe them too.

This is how anxiety has given me a sense of purpose.

I have learned to love and accept myself, to feel proud of what I am capable every day of overcoming.

I have learned to take deep breaths and to enjoy my own company.

I have learned the value of friendship — I am surrounded by people who support me and save me every day.

I have learned not to be ashamed — not one bit — of anything that I am.

The truth is my attempts to feel better about my anxiety have given me everything about my life that is beautiful.

Look at me. Look at what I have overcome. Look at how it's made me better, stronger. Look. Look at the resplendent life it has given me.

Unbreakable

You are not broken.

You are not broken. Life tosses you around, and sometimes everything hurts. It all feels scattered, fragmented, shattered.

Resist the temptation — the cheap satisfaction — of bundling everything up and slapping a sloppy label on it just to slip it into its fallacy of a category.

"I'm a mess." "Everything is horrible."

Step away from the surface, the ripples, the choppiness. Look at what's right at the center of you, at your core, radiating warmth.

Look at all the things you have survived.

Beautiful, untouchable, intact, sacred you. Indestructible.

You are not broken. What you are is unbreakable.

I am whole, and so are you.

Only You Can Help You

One of the biggest lies we tell ourselves is that someone else has the answers that we need.

That someone else has something we don't have — a wisdom, a perspective, a gift — that can save us.

I write a lot about the struggle inherent to life. There is so much pain in the world. Everyone is hurting. Many people — many, many people — reach out in a desperate search for answers.

It scares me to think what someone in my place could do to take advantage of people who are suffering.

I am adamantly against giving any form of personal advice. I write about things I've experienced and share what's worked for me, but this is completely different from directly weighing in on the life of a stranger, on a life I have zero context for.

You have all the answers. You have all the power. Do not squander it. Do not relinquish one bit of it. Do not give it away. Do not believe that someone else has everything figured out.

You have no idea what a mess I can be, with my inability to sleep and my anxiety, my tendency to go full tilt on everything and the sloppy rainbow love I splatter across white, pristine things. You don't see the middle of the night panic, the same mistakes I make over and over. *My god. I know this. I just wrote about this. Why am I doing it again?*

I don't have the answers that you need. But you do. You do, and as you stop looking outside of yourself and look inside, these answers will become increasingly clear.

I don't want my voice to ever drown out yours.

About the Author

Dushka Zapata has worked in communications for over twenty years, running agencies (such as Edelman and Ogilvy) and working with companies to develop their corporate strategy.

During this time she specialized in executive equity and media and presentation training. She helped people communicate better through key message refinement and consistency and coached them to smoothly manage difficult interviews with press during times of crisis.

Dushka is an executive coach and public speaker who imparts workshops about personal brand development. She has been hired for strategic alignment hiring, to coach and mentor high potential individuals, improve upon new business pitches, refine existing processes and galvanize a company's communication efforts.

Dushka is the author of nine books: "How to be Ferociously Happy", "Amateur, an inexpert, inexperienced, unauthoritative, enamored view of life", "A Spectacular Catastrophe and other things I recommend", "Your Seat Cushion is a Flotation Device", "Someone Destroyed My Rocket Ship and other havoc I have witnessed at the office", "How to Build a Pillow Fort and Other Valuable Life Lessons", "You Belong Everywhere and Other Things You'll Have to See for Yourself", "Love Yourself and Other Insurgent Acts That Recast Everything" and "Feelings are Fickle and Other Things I Wish Someone Had Told Me".

Dushka was recently named one of the top 25 innovators in her industry by The Holmes Report and regularly contributes to Quora, the question and answer site, where she has over 160 million views.

Made in United States
Troutdale, OR
12/16/2024

26630523R10224